THE SILVER FEATHER

**A young woman discovers that God hears
the silent screams of her heart.**

Mae Graybill Bachman

The Brethren Press, Elgin, Illinois

THE SILVER FEATHER

Cover Design by Wendell Mathews Associates

Library of Congress Cataloging in Publication Data

Bachman, Mae Graybill
  The silver feather.

  1.   Bachman, Mae Graybill.
  2.   Church of the Brethren—Biography. I. Title.
BX7843.B33A36   286'.5 [B]   80-27855
ISBN 0-87178-787-3

Published by The Brethren Press, Elgin, Illinois 60120

Printed in the United States of America

Dedicated

to Wendy Marie,
my youngest daughter
who devoted so much
time to the typing and
preparation of the manuscript.

Contents

Preface

Countless happenings in life demonstrate the unrefutable omnipotence, omniscience and omnipresence of God. There is no circuit or sphere where His Spirit cannot be found.

Innumerable biographies have been written of those who have erected monuments of faith upon our hearts and minds. Myriads of authors parade across the pages of history, and I must join them regardless of my listing. God's hand is upon mine, and I am compelled to write. In this exposé of the soul lies a deep religious undertow, the Spirit of God ever drawing and seeking to reconcile the human heart unto Himself.

The purpose of this book is to enable the reader to be cognizant of the persevering mercies of God, to stand in awesome wonder and behold His matchless love and grace, and to be assured that God can and does work miracles in the frailest of human beings.

No earthly ear hears or understands the "silent scream" as does our compassionate Lord.

Perhaps others will be able to relate with me in one aspect or another and thus be motivated to seek a deeper encounter with Him. Once you have yielded to His loving call you will never be the same again.

Mae Graybill Bachman
York, Pennsylvania
September 1980

Introduction

This book in a great measure is a true story. There are, however, some fictitious dates, names and places used in various parts of this narrative. I depended upon the Holy Spirit to draw from the archives of my mind these varied experiences and I am trusting Him to use them to magnify His wonderful Word.

This introduction may simplify the identity of each member of my family. They are named according to their place in order of birth. Each loved one was an integral part of my life.

Harry B. Graybill . . . . my beloved dad
Minnie B. Graybill . . . . my loving mother
Robert B. Graybill . . . . my brother — "Bob"
Myles B. Graybill . . . . my brother — Myles
Kathryn B. Graybill . . . . my sister — "Kitty"
Noah B. Graybill . . . . my brother — "Bill"
Mae B. Graybill
Elizabeth B. Graybill . . . . my sister — "Betty"

Chapter 1

In the Doctor's Satchel

At eight-twenty on a bright May morning a doctor quickly stepped out of his gray carriage, fastened the reins of his horse to a nearby hitching post and hurried with his satchel toward the two-story farmhouse.

The air was brisk and a steady volume of smoke ascended from the chimney. Tall fir trees towered like dignified sentinels on each side of the house, which appeared orderly and calm as it stood in the center of a tidy yard. Colorful little petunias embroidered the edges like a little girl's party apron. The windows were clean and shining, with blinds raised to invite the sun to share its warmth within. A lone exception was one room downstairs on the north side where the blinds were fully drawn. The persistent sun managed to peep through the cracks, penetrating the semi-darkness with long, golden fingers.

Most of the time this house was abounding with activity and laughter. But this Saturday morning one sensed an awesome silence mingled with expectancy. Even at age four, I was caught up in the excitement of this mysterious event!

This room on the north side was our parlor, opened only on Sunday or when company came. A wide hall separated the parlor from the kitchen. With tremendous curiosity I placed myself right outside the door leading into the parlor; here I had a good view as the door opened and closed.

It was obvious to me that the prim little parlor had been converted into a bedroom. The dark red rug was there with the three crocheted ovals to cover the worn places. The old organ was pushed against the wall. In the dim light I could see the neatly covered, old-fashioned bed and the night stand with its china bowl and pitcher. The matching chamber was tucked under a square-seated chair with a drop-lid. Over the seat and to the floor was a chintz curtain which enclosed the chamber completely.

The efficient nurse moved quickly between the parlor and the kitchen, carrying pans of steaming hot water and countless neatly folded white pads. As she whisked by me, closing the door firmly behind her, my anxiety mounted.

"If only I could peep in just once," I thought, as I pressed closer to the door. Antiseptic odors were filtering through the vent above the door. The voice of the doctor could be heard, and to my young mind he sounded rather cheerful. Although doctor visits were associated with grave illness or death, this one differed in that no one appeared sad or distressed. So I had to rely on my older sister's information, which seemed so brief.

"We are going to have a baby," she confided in a hushed voice as she helped me get dressed this morning.

"Why are shoestrings so tangly when we hurry?" I asked. She did not bother to answer, as her mind was elsewhere, but her deft movements told me that it was important as well as urgent to hurry quietly.

Sister Kathryn frequently assumed the role of an adult with me. I loved her. Because I was the baby of the family, she often mothered me, and I willingly obeyed her commands.

Now I was no longer the baby; someone was taking my place. I could be a big sister and act grown up too . . . help to dress and feed this sibling. Fantasies tumbled forth from my thoughts, questions mounted until I broke the silence with, "But Kathryn, where is the baby? How do we get it?"

As we reached the bottom step of the stairs, she leaned toward me and whispered, "It's in the doctor's satchel!" I could hardly comprehend this, but before I could resume the question Kathryn pressed a finger to her lips and underscored it with a warning look on her face. I had so many questions; if only Mother were well enough that I could ask her. The answers must wait, which was not a new experience for me.

Quietly I moved into the dimly lighted hall very near to the parlor door. No one could coax me to move. My little legs were signaling for a rest, but my curiosity and anticipation overruled. I daringly leaned my ear nearer to the crack of the door.

2

The door opened unexpectedly. Quickly I regained my upright position. In the dimness of the hall, the doctor did not notice me, but his satchel brushed against me as he made his way to the kitchen. To think that that mysterious satchel, which carried all kinds of things, had babies in it, too! I stared hopefully at the departing bag—no, it was tightly closed, so there was no chance of seeing a baby spilling out.

My brothers accompanied the doctor to the gate. I could see sister Kathryn setting the table, a happy expression on her face. The atmosphere of our home was a joyous one now. With renewed determination, I gently pulled on the parlor door; to my great delight it eased open about one-fourth inch.

Through the small opening I beheld an unforgettable scene. Standing on my toes so I could get a better view, I moved the door . . . it squeaked. I heard the soft murmur of voices. Daddy was bending over mother with tender concern written in his every look and action. Mother's face was all aglow. I did not notice her pallor or weariness, only the warmth of her smile to Daddy. This was enough to assure my heart that she was all right.

Mother was indeed thrilled. Was not her cup full and running over? Again the Lord had blessed her with a perfect baby—and a beautiful one, too! A bundle surely sent from Heaven, her hair borrowing the gold tints from the sun, her eyes reflecting the heaven's blue.

Unintentionally, I moved the door again. As it widened, Mother slowly turned her head, for even in the dim light of the hall she knew I was there. I waited breathlessly. Then I heard her say, "Mae, come and see what we have here. This is your new little sister. Her name is Elizabeth."

At the word "Mae," I started to tiptoe across the room. It was a hushed and reverent moment for me, broken only by irregular sucking noises. As I neared the bed, I was speechless. Right there at Mother's breast was the pinkest little baby I had ever seen. Although its eyes were closed, its mouth was eagerly drawing nourishment from Mother.

Mother's eyes were tenderly fixed on me. Finally she said in a soft voice, "Would you like to hold her?" Oh, how I wanted to hold her! Reading my thoughts, Mother added, "When she

3

is finished nursing you may hold her." It seemed forever till that great moment came. How warm and helpless she felt as she was placed in the curve of my young arms. There was so much to know about babies. I wondered how mothers knew it all. If Elizabeth had been in that satchel, I could not see any pinch marks or scratches.

That evening at the supper table I announced that I was a big sister. I was four fingers older than Elizabeth and I could do pretty many things — dry dishes, dust, pull weeds and run errands for others. My three brothers and sister laughed at me, but Daddy smiled and said, "Now, Mae, you can really help Mother, as she has to take it easy for several weeks." And help I did!

Elizabeth grew as a healthy, happy baby, quick to learn and imitate the actions of those about her. It seemed everything about her was lovable, even when she stamped her little feet in anger or frustration. Her cherub features encircled by golden curls drew affectionate attention from everyone.

In my own little girl's mind I thought Elizabeth (later shortened to Betty) was such a nice name. How I hated mine! Mamie Mae. When I was five, my brother Robert suggested we drop the "Mamie." From that time on I was called Mae, but still it was not a name I liked. Sometimes I would complain about my name, and Mother would try to comfort me by reminding me I was named after an aunt. Elizabeth could say my name quite well; I knew her "Mee" meant "Mae."

If I was jealous of Elizabeth in those tender years, I have no memory of being so. I stoutly defended her in her times of naughtiness. Her imagination knew no bounds. With her dolly and suitcase she would decide to move. A number of times she had the family frantically searching for her. These episodes usually ended in spankings. With patience and wisdom, Mother taught Elizabeth to find safer channels for her strong will and independent spirit.

4

Chapter 2

Our Family Faces a Move

The silence of night was intermittently broken by short, hacking coughs. Like all the typical nights of the last six months, Dad's cough had not improved. It was obvious that his health was rapidly declining. He had decided reluctantly to see a doctor.

Sleep had not overtaken me, and I vaguely heard my Mother whisper these incredible words: "Well, if it means you'll be well again, we will move to Florida."

Our bedroom door was always a little ajar, and frequently I would listen to their conversations. Patiently I waited for more words. Kathryn and I slept in a double bed; her soft, regular breathing proved she was asleep.

Scarcely daring to move, I wondered if Mother would continue her conversation. Having waited what seemed like a long, long time, I finally relaxed and sleep submerged my questioning thoughts.

Dawn had pushed back the darkness as I felt a persistent shake of my shoulder. It jarred me into consciousness. Kathryn was trying to awaken me. The brilliant shafts of sunlight pried my eyelids open. Lazily I moved out of bed. The rich aroma of fresh coffee drifted up the stairs. I washed, dressed and thoughtfully joined Mother in the kitchen.

With a smile she greeted me. "Well, good morning. Aren't you an early bird!"

Seating myself at the table I mumbled with my mouth full, "Muu huuh." Her pancakes were the best ever. The two she had placed on my plate were disappearing fast, the syrup was dripping from my chin. Last night's forbidden conversation surfaced in spite of Mother's serene countenance and the good food.

Removing a long-handled wooden spoon from the drawer, Mother turned, and her eyes rested on me. "Mae," she said,

5

"I believe you forgot to thank God for your meal. What if He would forget to bless us with food?"

I quickly licked the syrup off my hands and folded them in prayer. Although my lips clearly repeated the often-used "Thank you, Father, for this food, now bless it to Thy intended good," my heart and mind were still pursuing the big question: "Are we really going to move? I have lived in this house all of my four years!"

The regularity of "slurps" erupting from the hot pot of mush on the stove was broken into a bubbly noise as Mother stirred the thickening liquid. Humming softly, Mother's thoughts were turning pages. Last night's talk, with its decisions, deprived her of sleep. It was morning before she dozed off, only to be awakened at five thirty a.m. With a puzzled glance at me she wondered, "Why is little Mae strangely silent this morning? Had she heard last night's conversation that the doctor advised Dad to move to a warmer climate?"

Finding the silence unbearable, and my mind so full of questions, I slid off the chair from the table and moved over where I could see her face.

"Mama," I said, "do you think we'll ever move from here?" I knew better than to come right out and say, "Mama, where are we going?" Then she would know I had been listening again.

Her cheeks were flushed from the heat of the stove and dark wisps of hair curled softly on her moist temples and neck. Firmly and without emotion she replied, "Yes, likely we will move," then added, "but why do you ask?"

Skipping part of her question, I said, "But where will we move? Does Daddy really have to go away?"

"Yes," she answered wistfully, "and we must do everything we can to help him get well." Carefully she removed the large kettle of mush and placed it on a board at the sink to set. Oven-browned cornmeal was nourishing and, being a frugal family, we enjoyed this dish frequently, whether we ate it hot and soupy, with milk, or as solid slabs fried and served with pudding meats and molasses.

Now she turned her face to me and said, "Mae, sometimes God asks us to do difficult things, but He always promises to help us, and He is with us."

My parents taught us that God was always with us, even when we had lots of snow and could not leave our farm until we were shoveled out, or when the lightning struck our tree and barn. They still said, "He knew all about it, and He helped us escape harm."

Now we were going to move. I questioned, with some doubts, "Can God be everywhere all the time? But won't we leave God here if we move away, and who will protect us and help us then?"

"No, dear, God is everywhere, even way down south." Then Mother changed the subject. "Daddy will tell us all about it tonight at the supper table."

I could hardly wait until supper, but a number of hours had to be utilized before all the family came home.

I was trained early in life to help with various duties which had to be performed to keep a clean and neat home. I soon learned that Mother expected all of us children to do our chores well—"as unto the Lord." She taught us early that God could see everything we do and that He graded us accordingly.

The fear of God was instilled in our minds and hearts as early as I can remember. Although the love of God was also a twin truth, this teaching did not as greatly impress me or help me to control my motives and actions as did the fear of God's judgment.

Finally, it was time to take a nap. Little Mae did not enjoy this part of the day's activities, but it was a must; so reluctantly I made my way upstairs to my room. Downstairs it was very quiet and I knew Elizabeth and Mother were already napping.

The noisy buzz of a wasp between the blind and the window distracted my thoughts. "Why doesn't he stop banging his head on the blind?" I wondered. Turning my thoughts away from the tormented insect, I carefully crawled up on the foot end of the bed, trying not to disturb the covers. Curling into a small position, I soon began to daydream. How would it be to leave all the secret bird nests I had discovered and the pheasant nest in the corner of the corn field? I would miss my favorite nook behind the lilac bush where I would often hide after I had been punished for unruly behavior or neglected duties. Ex-

7

citing thoughts tumbled around like kaleidoscopic flashes, leaving no place for sleep.

It seemed like such a long time until I heard Mother call, "You may get up now."

I was eager to run out and meet Daddy as he wearily made his way toward the kitchen door. "Hello, Daddy," I greeted. He grasped my hand warmly. My short legs skipped in time with his long steps. He approached the old well pump and scrubbed his grimy hands with homemade soap. He vigorously splashed his face with the cold water, then swished dry with a towel. Stepping back to the walk, he grasped my hand and we entered the kitchen together.

I thought, "What a wonderful daddy I have?" He was the epitome of strength. I could not think of anything he could not do, and now Mother said he isn't well.

Anxiously I watched Mother's expression as she greeted him. Mother's actions were more expressive than her words.

"Well, how did it go with you today?"

Their eyes met in private communication. Then he said, in lighter tones, "I'm ready to eat a good meal, Mother."

Watching Daddy enjoy his meal and knowing we must have family devotions before Daddy would tell us about the plans he had almost took my appetite away.

Finally, his usual cup of hot water concluded his meal, and we were ready for our devotions. Reaching for the Bible, he opened it to Psalm 42 and clearly read the words aloud. At the eighth verse he paused a moment, then with tender but broken undertones he continued: "Yet the Lord will command his loving kindness in the daytime, and in the night his song shall be with me . . . "

We children kept our eyes on the floor and swallowed hard. It was not like Daddy to become so emotional. The noise of Mother's hanky could be heard in the solemn silence. Ending the scripture reading, Daddy led in family prayers. His words were almost tearful as he closed with the familiar Lord's Prayer. By this time my anxiety was at its peak.

I quickly straightened from my slouched position and sat erect in my chair, waiting. All but Mother, Dad and I had moved away from the table.

At last Daddy said, "Children, come back and sit down. I have something special to discuss with you."

Kathryn resumed her seat with the rest and whispered to me, "Oh, you must know something about this?" And I nodded my head emphatically and said, "Wait till you hear!" All eyes were focused on Daddy.

"Last week," he began, "I was with the doctor to check my cough. The doctor feels that a warmer climate is the only answer to better health. If I do not make this move soon, my lungs will not hold out. Mother and I have decided to move to Florida. The warmer days all year round will prevent the colds which I have in this colder climate."

"I'm sure," he continued, "you children will learn to like Florida as much as you do Pennsylvania. There is plenty of sunshine, year round bathing and fresh citrus fruit just for the picking."

None of us interrupted Daddy when he spoke, but there were all types of non-verbal signals given as we children anticipated the new life we soon were going to have in Florida.

Robert was the first to comment enthusiastically. "This sounds exciting! I think it will be good for all of us!"

Myles remained silent, obviously pondering both the pro and con implications of such a move.

Noah's face brightened as he visualized a daily swim. Under his breath he smugly proclaimed: "Just think! I won't have to take a bath down there!"

Being four summers old did not afford me an abundance of experience, but having developed a great deal of sensitivity, I quickly formulated my own set of impressions just from listening to the others. My emotions vacillated between fear and anticipation. I sensed Mother's lack of enthusiasm; was it with a shade of sadness?

Kathryn concluded the questions with this logical remark: "So we are all going to help build a new house!" Daddy had mentioned that we would temporarily have to stay in a much smaller house until the bungalow would be finished.

We children were chattering gaily as we left the table. Only Mother and Daddy were silent. Kathryn and I soon had the supper dishes put away, and each of us was digesting the news

9

in our own way.

In bed that night, whispered impressions and thoughts were shared. Lying close to my big sister, who conveyed no fear over this great move, brought a great measure of security and peace to my mind and heart.

Chapter 3

A Floating Home

It was early fall, and the days flew by before we realized it. Soon we were on our way to Baltimore to take a ship to Florida. All the preparations of moving such a distance took their toll. Daddy's cough had worsened. Even we children observed his declining health. Our beloved farm needed no real estate company to sell it. The little mailbox made like a windmill, with "H. B. Graybill" printed in large black letters, was removed. Sadly, we saw an ordinary box erected with another name on it.

Although Mother remained cheerful most of the time, she also shed many tears in the dark hours of the night. Leaving "home," where a book of experiences could be written, where all her relatives lived, and where her spiritual life was fed and nurtured in the disciplines of the Word, would mean a difficult time of readjustment. What a threat this new experience might prove to her family! To make new friends, find a good school and church, adjust to a different culture—all of this overwhelmed this quiet, shy country girl whose feet had only walked on Lancaster County soil.

Arriving in Baltimore we drove to Pier No. 4, where a huge ship was docked. All the confusion of getting our tickets, luggage and ourselves across the gangplank proved too upsetting for Elizabeth. At eleven months, strange faces, loud voices and unpleasant fish odors were pretty scary to her, even though she was nestled safely in Mother's arms.

Securely clasping Daddy's hand, I had to swallow hard to keep back the tears from creeping over the sills of my eyes. As we were being escorted to cabins, I began to feel a little safer. This enormous floating house was beautiful inside. Only the very rich folks could live in here. Daddy had previously shown us a picture of this ship. But how breathtaking to be inside! A neatly uniformed young man led us down a broad, richly-carpeted stair onto a lower floor, then through a long hall with doors which were numbered. Since I was learning to count, I figured this one must be ten, where the door was unlocked and we went inside. To my amazement I saw strange beds fastened to the walls—three, one on top of another, having narrow ladders to reach each one! In all there were six such beds. The young man continued, showing us where we could dress and bathe in privacy. Daddy thanked him, and he left. The room also contained small dressing tables with mirrors and chairs which had to be placed in grooves in the floor. How strange and unfamiliar everything seemed!

Elizabeth finally fell asleep. Mother had tenderly laid her in the middle of the bed. Then she deftly lifted the sheets and inspected the mattresses of each bunk bed. Finding no bugs, she neatly replaced the bedding. Six pairs of eyes watched her curiously, waiting for an explanation. Finally she turned and smiled, saying, "Well, everything looks pretty clean in here." Being an excellent housekeeper, she had no tolerance for dirt. Now she could relax and allow her family to fall asleep in these strange beds.

"Children, now you can get ready for bed." In no time at all we were in our nightclothes, gathered around our parents for our evening prayers. As we knelt on the soft, thick rug, we could feel the vibrations of many motors below us, also a gentle waving motion as our great ship was already ploughing through the deep seas.

It was difficult to concentrate on our devotions, or even to be fully aware of the serious tones Daddy's voice conveyed as he asked God to keep us in His love and care.

In spite of all the unfamiliar things about us, nature prevailed and I was off to dreamland.

Tuesday morning I awakened early. The dimly lighted room converged into reality. It was quiet. My top bunk gave me the privilege of touching the ceiling with either my fingers or my toes. I tried both, at the same time discovering that I had to crawl on my hands and knees to get over to the narrow ladder at the foot of my bed. Nearby was a round porthole which reminded me of Grandma's magnifying glass. I wondered, "Does it make the outside look larger or smaller? I will ask Daddy or Robert to lift me up so I can look through it for myself."

Looking over the edge of my bunk I whispered, "Is anyone else awake?" I would feel much more comfortable if some familiar voice would talk to me. I began to wonder if this was one of my "lost" dreams. I could never find my way to anyone I knew in my dreams. I was afraid of that kind of loneliness.

Carefully I crawled to the ladder and eased myself over, and down I went. Coming to the bunk below mine, I pulled the drawn curtains apart. Kathryn lay with her eyes shut; the baby softly curled by her side. No help from her. Descending to the floor bunk, I heard Daddy's muffled snore. Easing myself on the soft rug I proceeded across the room to the other three bunks. Just as I placed my feet on the first rung, the curtain opened above me. Noah's head popped out. Angrily he rasped, "What are you doing out of bed? Get back in bed or Elizabeth will waken and we'll all have to get up!" Four years my senior was enough to command my respect, so back to my ladder I went. Mother's voice gave me a start. "Mae, are you outside the curtain?"

"Yes," I whispered. "I can't sleep and I just want to be sure we are all here."

She sensed my need and added, "Open the curtain and crawl in here with us." I did not need further persuasion. How warm and secure I felt as I pressed close to her side.

Daddy awoke and turned, and teasingly he said, "Oh, do we have a new baby with us?"

"No," Mother replied, "just a lonely little girl who can't sleep."

The warm, clean smell of Mother's body, hinting of cashmere talc, brought a pleasing sense of comfort just for me. I laid there as still as I could, enjoying every moment of this intimacy we shared. I was still her very own little girl. For a period of time I lost the "oars of reality" and floated into an enchanted world. Before moving away, she gave me an affectionate kiss and whispered, "We must get up or we will miss our breakfast."

A muffled "Din-nggg" sounded through the room to remind us of the first call for breakfast. Then followed a gentle tap on the door. In her robe Mother carefully released the lock on the door and eased it open. A narrow shaft of light cut into the semi-darkness of our room.

"Good morning, Ma'am. Breakfast will be served from seven to nine-thirty on the second deck."

It was the same voice that provided all the information we needed to get settled last night.

"Here's Miss Torie. She's the nursemaid on this deck and she will be glad to mind the children should they become ill or require any special attention."

Her neat uniform and congenial yet professional manner left no doubts in our minds that she was well aware of each passenger assigned to her care.

In no time at all we were dressed and told to wait out in the corridor. Dad and Mother soon joined us and instructed us to behave and be quiet and polite. Daddy knew where to go, so all seven of us followed in duck-like fashion, with Mother at the end, gently guiding little Elizabeth. It seemed like an endless hall, and Elizabeth believed each door we passed was the entrance to the breakfast room. A few feet ahead Daddy paused, then descended a short stairway. This stair opened to a spacious dining room.

Selecting a large enough table, Daddy beckoned us to come and be seated. Even Elizabeth had her own high chair. My chair was adjustable, so I sat like a big lady next to Daddy.

This brilliant, golden room made us less aware that we were minus nature's contributions such as the sun and clean fresh air. Like our beds and chairs, our dishes were all placed in grooves. The meal was unlike any I had ever eaten. We shared sips and samples of various foods and found all this so exciting! Completely satisfied and filled, we filed back to our room. Arriving at our cabin we noticed two of us missing—Robert and Myles. They had likely taken off to make discoveries of their own.

Mother was disheartened to return to our room and find that our beds were made. What must that maid think of her. Was she a sloppy housekeeper? It wasn't long until Mother learned it was the duty of the maid to make beds.

Once again Daddy led us through the long hall. This time

we turned right and moved on through double doors which abruptly led to a broad stairway. Looking up, we could see the blue sky. Daddy said we were going up on the top deck! The steps were carpeted but seemed endless. Reaching the top was breathtaking.

With a dash I was off to explore, but not far; I heard Daddy's voice remind me to stay close by. Never had my eyes beheld such a vast amount of water. The sun was so bright that it glistened like a mirror on the quiet seas. A sturdy rail protected the passengers as we leaned over to watch the schools of fish and the fascinating wake which trailed our ship.

"Daddy," I cried in dismay, "where are the trees, and the hills? Did the sea swallow them up? Do you think Jonah's whale could be down there? Could our ship turn over in all this water? Could? Could . . . ?"

"Now, wait a minute, Mae, one question at a time." He caught my hidden fears and matter of factly said, "First, you need not be afraid, this is one of the safest ships made. It can travel on the deepest seas and stand weeks of travel without refueling."

"You see," lifting me up in his arms, he pointed to a faroff blurred line, "over there is land." The deep blue sea merged into a silver line, and it appeared rounded. The blue sky seemed to drop its clouds as though swallowed up by the sea. "Distance makes land disappear."

"There," he continued, "are white objects moving up and down. They are called porpoises. They have fun jumping up above the surface like that. Their bellies are white, and they resent when ships pass by and churn the water. As for whales, there could be some far out in the sea, but Jonah's whale no doubt has died long ago."

Reassured by Daddy's calm answers, my attention was diverted to discovering all kinds of interesting things on deck. There were big circles like tires that Dad called life preservers. The long, comfortable deck chairs had blankets and pillows. People were sitting or lying around in the sun. There were two strangely dressed ladies with white bands over their foreheads and black head capes and dresses. They smiled and spoke softly to one another. Crosses hung from their necks on long chains. Mother called them "Nuns." Also, there was a joyful little group of people in a circle, all playing various kinds of musical instruments. Kathryn said they might be gypsies. Later I heard a man say they were Italian musicians (from a musical group). This was the most interesting adventure I ever had. It was more fun than swimming in the creek at home.

Chapter 4

Fascinating But Forbidden

Three days passed, and each one provided all kinds of excitement and fun. My parents permitted me to tag along with any of the older siblings as long as I "was a good girl." Kathryn and I would walk all around the second deck. Once I almost stepped into an open "manhole!" Sometimes their lids would suddenly pop up and a nice sailor would crawl up on deck. I thought they were playing "Jack in the Box." Once a sailor motioned to me to come nearer as he stood halfway out of the hole. Somewhat cautiously and shyly I stepped within four feet. He smiled and said, "What is your name?" He looked so kindly at me he did not seem like a stranger. Taking one step closer, I answered brightly, "My name is Mae, I was born in May, and my birthday is in May."

"Oh, how nice, and how old are you?" he questioned.

With four fingers held up, I answered, "Can you count?"

"Yes," he chuckled. "so you are four and I am twenty-four. Next time I see you here I will have a present for you." With that he threw a handful of peanuts at my feet and disappeared into the "manhole." The heavy metal lid closed after him.

Mother looked worried when I related the incident to her. We were warned not to make friends with strangers. Kathryn was admonished for letting me wander away from her side.

That evening after dinner the family assembled on deck to find the sailor that I had told them about. Daddy cast a wary eye at the metal caps scattered over the deck board. A few hops and skips ahead, I recognized the hole. Pointing to it, I cried, "That's the one 'Mr. Jack in the Box' came up from!"

Daddy walked over nearer the hole, stared a bit, then turned to us and said, "There's a very slim chance you'll see him again with over a hundred sailors on this ship." A moment later the lid opened. Up and out crawled "Mr. Jack."

"Howdy, folks," he addressed us. "Nice evening to be strolling the deck." Not waiting for an answer, he added, "Sure hope the weather continues to favor us."

Astounded at the sudden appearance of my sailor friend, Daddy gave him a short nod and waited.

"Mae and I have become acquainted. Somehow she seemed to understand I am homesick for my family and friends. I've been on board for nine months."

Daddy nodded sympathetically and said, "Mae seems to like everyone and makes friends easily."

With an apprehensive glance at Mother, my newfound friend quickly added, "I hope I didn't cause you any concern. Mae's friendliness cheered me, and I promised her a present the next time we met, so here it is." Leaning forward, he handed me a white paper bag and once again disappeared into the hole. The metal lid fell into its place with a noisy clang. Gingerly I opened the bag and discovered to my great delight a darling Cupie doll!

Hugging the doll, I exclaimed in dismay, "Oh, dear, I do hope I shall see him again to say 'Thank you' for such a nice present."

At ten o'clock a.m. each day the captain would announce over the loudspeaker all the news and weather conditions, as well as port stops and directions of our traveling courses. He would conclude the announcements with all the entertainments which were offered to passengers for that day and night. These entertainments consisted mostly of movies, shows, ballroom dancing and jazz band performances.

Being brought up to believe that God's people do not conform to the world, we naturally saw all this as worldly entertainment. This was not for Christian people. In my heart, along with the rest of my brothers and sisters, were longing desires to see for myself these sinful indulgences of dancing and watching pictures flashing off and on the screens.

Sometimes I lingered at the French doors which led into the ballroom and stage auditorium, hopeful that someone would open that door just a crack so I could satisfy my curiosity.

One day it rained until four in the afternoon. My parents returned to our room to write letters shortly after lunch, believing I was with the older ones. But I had hidden in the rest rooms until the passageway was clear. Carefully I made my way back to the large curtained French doors. If only they would move just a wee bit, then I could see inside. It took courage to push one door, but my curiosity compelled me, and push I did. With ease the door silently swung inward. Once inside I stepped forward and the door swung back into place. There I was wide-eyed and overwhelmed! Like a fleeting shadow, I tucked myself between the huge folds of a purple velvet curtain which hung from the ceiling to the floor. Scarcely breathing I waited, watched and listened.

The music sounded soft and pleasant. The ceiling was brilliantly lighted with wheel-like fixtures adorned with countless prisms of glass reflecting rainbow colors. On the right side of the musicians were couples sitting at tables drinking from tall glasses. In the middle of the floor was a given place to dance. It was the dancing that captured my attention. As I watched their graceful movements, I wondered if the ladies had lost the tops of their dresses. Didn't their mamas tell them to use a safety pin when a dress does not close properly? In spite of their immodesty, I was fascinated and could not keep from staring. Enthralled with their harmonious movements and graceful beauty, I was unprepared for the startling interruption.

A large black hand gripped my shoulder. Scarcely daring to move, I heard a deep voice say, "Chile, why you all hid'en hyeah?"

Daring to tilt my head, I found the big hand attached to a tall, uniformed man. Never had I been that close to a Negro. What might he do with me? Would he throw me in one of those dark holes or maybe into the greedy waves that lashed so noisily against our ship's sides? Wordlessly I waited, too frightened to realize that he had asked me a question. My enchanting movements vanished, I was faced with stark reality!

In a more gentle tone I heard the man ask, "Wheah ah youah' pa'ents?"

My jaw felt stiff and I could only stutter, "I . . . I . . . don't know."

"Come," he continued, leading me out of the spacious ball-

19

room and firmly holding my hand. "We will repoa't to de cap'tin, and he will locate youah pa'ents." How long and dark the hall appeared as I walked like a mannequin beside him.

We had only gone a short distance when we met Robert hurrying toward us. "There you are! Where have you been? We were all hunting for you all over the place."

The officer interrupted Robert, saying, "I discove'ed huh hid'en in de ballroom b'tween de folded cut'ins while mak'in my roun's."

Wriggling my hand free from the officer, I quickly ran to Robert's side and grasped his hand. Still fearful, yet wanting to convince the officer, I said boldly, "He's my big brother."

"Yeh . . ." he replied with a smile, "I ken see he is. Now yo' stay close to him, hyeah?" Then, slowly turning, he moved down the passageway.

Robert did not need to remind me that punishment was my just lot. I meekly accepted my parents' rules. They rarely changed them. Discipline surely follows disobedience. In my mind anything my parents would do would be better than being thrown into a dark hole or the fierce rolling waves, as my imagination threatened could have happened!

Later when I told Mother how frightened I was, she reassured me that the officer was really a kind person, and he was only doing his duty.

Missing an ice cream treat and going to bed earlier than usual gave me plenty of time to regret my naughtiness, also to reflect on my foolish fears about the officer's possibility of harming me. None of these left so great an impression as the dazzling sight of those ladies dancing in the ballroom.

Chapter 5

Lessons in Survival

The fourth night of sea traveling came all too soon. We had three more days and we would arrive in Florida. Sea travel proved a learning experience for all of us. Wednesday's day of rain ended in late afternoon. Broken clouds spanned out, nudging each other joyously as they moved southward. The late sun spangled the decks with shimmering droplets left by the late dismal downpour. Everyone welcomed the sun.

After dinner our family spent several hours on Deck Number Two. Here passengers met to visit, or stroll, or play games. Some of us shared devotions together, thus deepening our friendships and strengthening our faith in God. Up here the golden splendored sunsets were breathtakingly beautiful. But the nights were exquisite, like embroidered canopies of navy blue with an ice white moon encompassed by diamond French knots.

On one of such nights I heard my Daddy whisper to Mother, "See, what God hath wrought!"

We docked in Jacksonville, Florida, on a Monday morning. Loudspeakers were screeching directions, information and names. Utter confusion was the order: tearful goodbyes, misplaced baggage, lost children and the sheer excitement to get ashore.

Calmly Daddy directed us to our designated gangplank. There, sure enough, stood our black Maxwell. It had come along with us, parked in the storage garage of the ship.

How strange to stand on firm ground again! After we were packed in the car we were soon heading toward Sebring. Our car was groaning under its luggage-laden sides, top and rear. There were eight of us to occupy the two seats, but to relieve the situation a little there was a small stool placed on the floor behind the front seat. Many times I occupied that seat.

After several hours of cramped traveling in ninety-five

degree heat, tempers became short and Elizabeth started to whimper. Robert complained that we girls stopped at every "dog house" as an excuse to get out and run around a bit. This of course hindered our speed to reach Sebring by nightfall. By eleven o'clock p.m. we pulled into a would-be driveway. Only deep ruts in the sand directed our way. Our Maxwell gave one choking cough and halted with a jerk. Although travel-worn, our anticipation to see our new home prevailed. Daddy sensed the excitement and reminded us to take it easy and to help carry the luggage inside.

Since it was almost midnight, we could barely see the small frame dwelling we were to call home. We practically fell out of the car. With a key Daddy preceded us, opening the narrow door so we each could enter, laden as we were with luggage. After some groping around, Daddy discovered a small dusty bulb hanging from the center of the room. The room had small doors and openings which gaped darkly at us. There was no real furniture except an old bed with a urine-soaked mattress. A built-in stove reeking of stale bacon fat all spoke loudly for its former occupants' neglect. A few broken boards nailed above a black sink claimed the title of a pantry.

Mother's dismay could not be hidden. We gathered in a desolate group. No one dared to sit down on the bed or the floor. Mother and Daddy held a consultation in Pennsylvania Dutch, their customary method of conversation when we children were not to understand what was being said.

Finally, Daddy said, "Robert, go out and bring all those newspapers in that we brought along. We will lay them on the floor, and we'll settle here for the night."

Wearily Robert returned with an armload of papers. Daddy was an avid news reader and we had collected quite a number. While the papers were being spread around on the floor, Mother had unpacked some covers and pillows. These were laid on top, and in no time at all we nestled down for the night. Exhausted, we slept, unaware of the nocturnal invaders who inhabited this house before we came.

A month of cramped living taught us many valuable lessons — patience being the foremost. We quickly scrubbed and cleaned the house, if it could be called a house.

Mosquitos, gnats, ants, hard-backed roaches, not to mention poisonous spiders, made everyday a survival operation. They seemed to fatten on our flesh! Within a few weeks, we younger ones broke out in ugly sores. These were like tiny volcanoes oozing pus.

Then there was the hookworm for which we had to be tested twice a year by stool examinations. Fortunately, we escaped the hookworm infection. The intense heat, strange drinking water and varied acid fruits which we consumed in abundance took their toll on our plumbing and piping systems. It took at least six months for our digestive systems to accept the new diets and for our skins to adapt to the scorching sun rays. But in time we all had excellent tans and healthy complexions.

Daddy's health definitely was improving. He had gained weight, and seldom would we hear him cough. Mother was so thankful for Dad's restored health that she made every effort to hide periods of homesickness. Letters were a great source of comfort to her. When she was not occupied with housework, she could be seen at the kitchen table writing letters.

In less than a year we had moved into the nicest kind of home, as a matter of fact right next door to our first trying residence! It was a bungalow with a large fireplace that afforded comforting heat on damp, chilly mornings. Mother would place interesting things on the mantle which would capture our attention. She loved birds, plants and flowers.

I made a hobby of collecting small things, such as pine cones and needles, birds' eggs that fell to the ground, sea shells and countless other items. Pine needles could be used in making all kinds of interesting objects. In daily vacation Bible school I learned how to weave mats and baskets. We gave many of these to relatives and friends when they visited us.

We had various pine and citrus trees all about us. Even a banana tree was planted near the back porch. It spread its broad foliage like an umbrella of shade. It was my tree, given to me on my sixth birthday. When it was fully matured, it bore ladyfinger bananas. What a delight to enjoy the fruit of one's own banana tree!

Sebring was a tourist town. When we settled here, it was

small in size, perhaps five hundred people. It was built like a wheel; the northerners were settled on the inside of the rim, and the blacks and Florida "Crackers" lived on the outer edge.

The Ku Klux Klan threw its weight around, threatening and daring the blacks to make a mistake. Their monthly rituals were weird and awesome. They claimed to tar and feather their culprits who were delinquent. Their flaming torches and burning crosses put terror in some hearts. As children, we did not understand their rights and claims, but we suffered from nightmares. We smelled burning flesh, whether human or animal we could not tell. We heard their angry voices and watched their ghostly figures parade around.

Daddy would shake his head at such rituals and remind us, "We are God's people, and we would not participate in such wickedness. We have civil officers to handle the persons who have committed crimes."

One time when I was returning home from an errand for Mother I met a very tall white man, his skin bronzed and toughened by outdoor activity. He lumbered slowly by me. I had to look up to see a long-bladed knife fastened in a leather holder to his belt.

A black man was cautiously approaching us. The sidewalk was wide enough for each to pass. As the two figures neared, the black man slowed his step, swaggering to the left. The white man moved in the same direction and blocked the other's way.

Within six feet, I stood frozen to the spot as I watched the white man carefully remove the long-bladed knife. His tobacco stained lips poured forth profanity in rasping, gutteral sounds.

Rolling his eyes back in his head, the black man muttered, "Oh, Lawdie," as the shiny blade neared his throat. Clumsily he lurched backward and stumbled off the pavement, still gasping, "Lawdie, Lawdie."

The white man replaced his knife and defiantly moved on. With trembling limbs, I crossed the street and willed my legs to run. Pale and winded, I finally reached home. How safe and secure it was there. Anxiously, Mother eyed me, waiting for me to calm down and catch my breath and explain why I was so frightened.

Later, at the supper table, Mother related my story, but in a calm and casual manner. Wisely, she ended with, "Daddy, these skirmishes only happen between the blacks and the Florida 'Crackers,' don't they?"

"Yes," he replied; "The 'Crackers' will never permit the blacks to feel equal to the white man."

This was my first introduction to racial conflicts. Living in Florida as a resident, one soon became aware of the injustice and cruelty of racial conflicts and prejudice.

Chapter 6

Sore Thumbs and Other Joys

We children adjusted well to the southern culture. Even the Pennsylvania Dutch dialect, for which we were frequently teased and identified as "Dutchmen," was lost. Sooner than we realized our vocabulary acquired "yo'all," "younder," and many other colloquialisms.

Elizabeth was two when Daddy decided that our family of eight must have a larger house. Both parents drew the original plans, then with professional help a blueprint was made. The eight room, two-story house was to be built right next door to the bungalow where we were living. It was strange to learn that no one had basements in our town. The sand-surfaced earth with its moisture was unsuitable for basements. So foundations were built above the sand supported by blocks or walls.

What an exciting time as we children would dream, plan and visualize our new home. Two bathrooms were a luxury, one upstairs and one on the first floor. This meant less arguments, and fewer "jigs" outside the bathroom door! We were even allowed to hammer the laths on the walls. It was a family project, and every one of us had a part to fill. There were pretty many sore thumbs as we were learning to hammer the nails straight into the laths. Daddy was particular, so it required plenty of practice. Each day the framework took on more of a house pattern.

In less than eight weeks we could move into our new, if unfinished, house. We labored literally without rest, aided by our kind neighbors who pitched in to help from time to time. Fresh paint was everywhere. This required constant reminders from Mother like, "Hands off! Take off your shoes and empty the sand before you come in! Please stop playing with that electric light switch! Lift your chairs, don't drag them around." Countless other admonitions were given to remind us that the new house must be cared for and that it did not come to us easily.

By this time I was a well adjusted first grader. Learning was a happy experience for me. I could come home and play school with Elizabeth as my pupil. She was quick to learn and accepted my pretended role as a teacher. She had quite a repertoire of rhymes and songs she had learned in Sunday school.

At the end of my first year my report card brought a recommendation from my teacher. It was suggested to my parents that I was capable of moving into the third grade. My mother was not so sure about the wisdom of such a promotion, but Daddy felt it was advantageous because I was so eager to learn. So my second year was really a third year of education.

The pupils with the highest grades were offered a free airplane trip and a citation. This was indeed an exciting reward to attain. Although I was numbered on this achievement list, my dear mother did not permit me to accept the plane trip. I am unable to explain why she opposed the plane ride. Perhaps the decision was governed by her fear for my safety or concern for my heart condition. This affliction was discovered at birth. My parents were frequently concerned, as it was especially noticeable to them after I exercised vigorously. I was unaware of any abnormality accepting myself as I was. I had no fears concerning my heart, so I took all their warnings lightly. High strung and energetic, I moved into adolescence a fairly healthy person. I won prizes for running, and swimming was my greatest pleasure.

Mother once informed me that if I took care of myself I could probably live to be an old lady. She also reminded me that God has our days numbered and He also knows when we would die. But *we* can hasten our death and hinder His plans by disobedience to His laws.

Chapter 7

Blessings on My Head

When the Depression of the 1930s hit Florida, we all experienced a difference in lifestyle. We could only afford meat once a week. There were less eggs to be used, and we drank watered-down milk. Garden provisions were ample so we did not really suffer. Daddy daily thanked the Lord for the abundant supply the garden provided. Dad's check was almost elastic, but still it did not cover all our expenses. A family of eight had many needs.

One day Mother firmly announced that she could help meet expenses by taking in washing. Soon our wash lines advertised her efforts with bright colors and various sizes of garments plus snowy white linens.

Kathryn and I were Mother's helpers. We turned many hours of labor into hilarious moments and fun. We made up a game called "describe the person who wears this."

Mother earned the reputation for having the whitest wash in town. She was meticulous with white shirts. Not the smallest wrinkle was allowed when we pressed them. This was an art in itself. The starch dipped collars and cuffs must appear like a professional job.

I was elected to deliver the laundry to the persons who did not or could not come for their belongings. Mother would neatly lay the folded laundry in a basket and place it on a small wagon. I would carefully pull the wagon to each owner's home, deliver the wash, collect the pay, and return home again. This chore taught me to communicate with adults, to understand and accept their personalities just as they were.

This responsibility proved to be a rewarding one for me. Sometimes I would receive a goodie to eat or more often a nickel or a dime. On special days I would be rewarded with a dollar. Money was scarce and it was really exciting to receive that much! I would promptly put it in the bank, occasionally making an exception. If I was clever enough, I could manage to hide a small amount which was later used to buy Mother a present. She knew all about my little tricks, but she never let on that she knew. She would act surprised and touched, which made my giving pure enjoyment.

She washed for one couple who made a lasting impression on my life. They resided in the parsonage close to our church. Reverend J. H. Moore and his wife were an elderly couple and very frail. Their physical frailness did not hinder a beautiful Christian testimony.

Sister Moore, as we respectfully addressed her, was pitifully thin. I was sure a brisk wind could blow her away. Her lucent face was so pale. Her large dark eyes were planted deeply, giving one an impression of looking into eternity, with an acquiescent spirit awaiting its flight. In spite of her fragile frame she moved about in a dignified manner. Thick silver braids adorned her head like a queenly crown. Perhaps her abundant head of hair spoke of former years of vibrant health and vitality.

Sister Moore always wore white dresses made of the finest fabrics and adorned with exquisite embroidery. Her high collars were edged with delicate laces. Long sleeves and ankle-length hems denoted her modest taste and also enhanced her ethereal appearance. When she moved about I caught the scent of violet sachet.

I was sensitive to spiritual things, and I was aware of God's Presence in this comfortable home. I wondered if Heaven would smell of violets and herbal teas.

Tapping lightly on their screen door, I would patiently wait to hear Sister Moore's thin voice say, "Come in." It was cool and dark inside, the drapes being drawn to prevent the sun's heat.

I carefully lifted the basket from the wagon, and once inside I knew where to place it. Painstakingly she would lay each piece on the table in little heaps. Slowly turning to me with a satisfied smile, she would motion me toward the study and in a barely audible voice I would hear, "Brother Moore is waiting for you."

This was an awesome experience, my visit with Brother

Moore. Timidly I walked across the hall and waited in the doorway of his study. Hearing my steps, he summoned me to enter. I could smell the books, both old and new, that lined the walls and littered his desk and table. Papers were stacked here and there, indicating much typing, for he was an author as well as a minister. No doubt these were parts of his manuscripts. This study was the most peaceful place on earth.

Brother Moore always offered me peppermints from a seemingly bottomless jar. After selecting one I would clutch it tightly in my sweaty little hand and say, "Thank you." He would take his slippered foot and push the hassock towards me and invite me to sit down. After several visits I shyly took my seat without hesitation. My thoughts took a special path when I visited here, "Was Brother Moore like God?" I wondered. His ways were so kind and unchangeable. "I wish I could be so kind and good all the time." In this room I was so aware of being two different people. The "nicest Mae" would dominate my actions here.

Brother Moore was very old. His voice seemed to rumble from under his long white beard which lay neatly on his chest. Age softened the lines of his angular features. Intelligence marked his high brow which was free of wrinkles in spite of years of vicissitudes and trials.

Heavy white brows intensified his penetrating eyes. I fearfully hoped he could not see the "ugly Mae" I knew I could be. His large hands had a patterned network of blue tracings which inched their way up under his sleeves. They were quiet hands and gentle, too.

I felt so pious in his presence. There was no need to talk, so I sat and waited for him to speak. Somehow I sensed his ageless wisdom and was dumb before it, knowing I was in a Godly presence. He never referred to my personal sinful state, yet I was keenly aware that I was a sinner, young as I was.

During our visit he would inquire about the health of my family or remark about the weather. But always he showed real concern about his wife's failing health. After general remarks, he would speak more profoundly in this manner.

"Make use of time, little one, you'll soon be old. The Lord may come soon, are you ready to meet Him?" or "God is everywhere and no secret can be hidden from Him" and "Guard your reputation more carefully than possessions." These were priceless jewels from his spiritual inheritance which he so graciously shared with me. I enjoyed these remarks more than when he read the scriptures to me.

After some conversation he would sigh deeply, turn towards the desk and remove a dime from the desk drawer and hand it to me, indicating our visit was over. In a soft whisper I thanked him and tiptoed out into the brilliant sun. Only then would I remember to lick the "mat of goo" that was once a fresh peppermint patty from my hand.

There was one visit that was different from all the rest. After seating myself on the hassock with the mint clutched in my hand, I waited for the usual words of wisdom, then my reward of a dime, and I would be on my way again.

But the usual words were not forthcoming . . . only a strange period of silence. Brother Moore's eyes were closed. I grew a bit weary of waiting what seemed like the longest time. Could I sneak a nibble from my mint while his eyes are closed? Temptation prevailed and I had just broken off a piece and was whirling it under my tongue when I noticed he was watching me. Triple lines broke at the corners of his eyes. He was smiling, then he said, "Child, eat all of it, before it melts. Pleasures like sweet mints soon pass away." Embarrassed, I popped the rest of the melting mint in my mouth, letting it slowly dissolve as I waited for him to speak again.

He finally startled me with this question: "What would you like to do when you grow up?"

I loved to act and secretly imagined perhaps someday I could be a famous actress who would dance and sing. I loved to draw and paint, and frequently dreamed of having a fine set of oil paints and an easel. There were times when I was sure I would become a doctor or a nurse. I was sympathetic and naturally took to helping people if I could when they were injured or hurt. I excelled in art and health in school.

I did not know how to answer such a question. To be educated was costly, and who would be interested in such dreams? Hesitantly, I answered, "Well, I'm not sure what I'd like to do when I grow up. I like to draw a lot . . . "

Brother Moore appeared not to be listening. My thoughts continued to dribble like a leaky faucet. "Is he asleep again? Did he forget about the dime? Were his lips moving in prayer?" . . . on and on they trickled . . . "I wonder if he looks like Moses, or maybe Abraham?" Then I was glad I didn't tell him I wanted to be an actress. That was not considered Christian practice.

Once again his eyes were open and were thoughtfully focusing on me, "Child, I will pray for you and ask God to pour special blessings on your head."

In a small voice I said, "Thank you, but what does special blessings on your head mean?"

From down under his beard I heard him reply, "Well, dear child, I have observed that you are endowed with a number of talents. God would have you develop and use them to serve Him in a fuller measure."

I did not fully comprehend the meaning of his words, but it was fine with me if my dreams came true. With these remarks he leaned forward and placed his hands upon my head. Closing my eyes, I waited for his prayer.

"Dear Heavenly Father," he prayed, "in Thy great mercy keep Thy loving hand upon this child. May she learn to know You as her personal Saviour. May all the talents that are hers be used to honor Thee. Lead her in Thy way and will and make her life a blessing to others. Amen, Amen."

Outwardly I was motionless. Inwardly a beam of light had probed the deeper recesses of my soul, exposing the real me. A deep yearning filled my whole being, a yearning to be one person, not two as I knew myself to be. My longings for understanding were wordless, but my eyes never left Brother Moore's kind face.

Gently, he asked, "Do you have a question?" That moment of conflict was broken. I was unable to surface my struggle, and spread it out before such a Godly person. How could he understand?

Shuffling my thoughts, I came up with, "No . . . no . . . Brother Moore, I . . . I hardly know what to say. Sometimes I wish I would know God like you do."

Laying his hand on the Bible, he said, "Study this book

daily, and God will tell you all you want to know about Himself."

Sighing softly, he began to read, and I quietly arose and made my way out of the house. Mechanically I pulled the wagon towards home.

The beams of those golden moments were like hidden investments kept in the "trust account" of my heart. I did not realize their worth. In due time they provided dividends and benefits which were beyond explanation.

Chapter 8

Hurricane Horror

Hurricanes were a frequent threat to the Florida coast in the fall of the year. Since Sebring was located so centrally in the state, it was seldom hit severely by these devastating winds. But in the year of 1928 we had a hurricane that played havoc. It was a fearful experience!

Elizabeth was in the first grade that year, and I was a sixth grader. We often experienced high winds so I was not unduly frightened over the weather. However, after the storm broke in fury upon us, I noticed my teacher's concern. As she rushed to close the large windows, she loudly ordered us to quickly form a line and move out into the hall. Before every child had left the room, we heard a crashing sound. Panes of glass were splintering the air, and some of the children were cut and bleeding. Outside in the hall, a hysterical child was seeking her sister. I worked my way through the cringing crowd and saw Elizabeth. I rushed over to comfort her as she held out her arms to me. Pandemonium broke loose as we all wildly headed for the stairs. Tumbling over each other down the steps, we jammed the entrance of the first floor. I clutched Elizabeth's hand tightly as she pressed close to me. Lightning like forked tongues blazed, snapped and licked at the walls of the dim halls, only to vanish, leaving us trembling with the sound of earth-shaking thunder. Frozen with fear we were packed in the hallway, waiting for orders from the principal. In a loud voice, he instructed us to form human chains. For each street called, an older student clasped the hand of a younger one and moved out into the storm towards the designated streets. We literally clung to fences, trees and street posts as we deposited each child to his or her home safely. Mothers waited anxiously to rescue their children as they came by.

Roofs from various sheds and poorly constructed buildings were somersaulting down streets and across lawns. Little

Elizabeth could scarcely whimper for need of a breath. Wide-eyed, she moved her little legs, stumbling along beside me. Twigs and small branches pelted our faces. Telephone poles swayed haphazardly as the frenzied winds tore around them. As I desperately hurried on, I whimpered to myself, "Is God in all this?"

At last it was our turn to rush for shelter. Looking like kittens rescued from a well, we dashed toward our porch. I dragged little Elizabeth across the twenty-foot yard and up on the porch. Mother was there waiting for us. Her skirts were wet, and her long white apron, ballooned by the wind, descended like a wet tent on our heads. Her arms enfolded us as she hurriedly pushed us inside. Her little white prayer veil was drooping as it clung to her hair. I shall always remember her face. Her usually tender blue eyes were bright with anxiety, and her flushed cheeks heightened the expression she was trying so hard to hide.

I sensed her fear, and the danger of the whole experience suddenly hit me. Mother helped us change into dry clothes, constantly talking in a forced, cheerful way. Elizabeth's fear soon subsided, comforted by Mother's presence, but I trembled and shivered as I ran from window to window, watching torrents of rain pour from our roof spouts.

I had to talk; it helped somehow. I started a barrage of questions. "Mother, where is Daddy? Why doesn't he come home? Will Kathryn stay at Marian's house tonight?" (Marian was her best friend, and lived two blocks away.) "When will the boys be home? Can the storm blow our pine trees over?" My inquisitive mind had a temporary reprieve by the noisy entrance of my daddy and three drenched brothers as they talked excitedly about the storm.

Suddenly we heard a horrendous thundering noise. We rushed to the kitchen window and stared in amazement. It was like a fairy tale. There before us was our pastor's house, rolling and tumbling down the street, tossed about like a mere matchbox! We could not believe our eyes. In two breaths of time, an ear-splitting crash followed. The earth trembled for a moment, then only the awesome havoc of the elements could be heard. The wild winds tore at our roof viciously. Dashing to the rear window, I saw the tallest pine tree lying only a few feet from our house. Shorn of its glory, it lay there all splintered and broken. Paralyzing fear gripped me. Perhaps I screamed; I am not sure what happened. The next thing I knew I was nestled on Daddy's lap. His strong warm arm encircled me. The steady cadence of his heart brought a measure of calmness and security to me as he gently stroked my hair.

Slowly, I emerged from my prison of fear. Glancing up into his face, I saw assurance and a trusting heart. Mother was softly singing Elizabeth's favorite nursery rhyme as she rocked her to and fro.

Daddy whispered in my ear, "Are you all right now?"

Nodding yes, I thought, "There's nowhere else I could be safer in such a storm." After a time, I broke the silence. "Daddy, do you think my friend Elaine was in her house when it tumbled down our street? Do you think she is still alive? If she is alive, where will they live since they have no house?" Elaine Forest was my dearest friend, and her daddy was our pastor.

In a quiet tone Daddy answered my questions. "I am not able to say where Elaine and her parents are now, but very likely they are safe in the house which stands in the rear of their yard."

Interrupting him, I said, "Why did our tallest pine tree fall over?"

He continued. "Sometimes trees are very rotten inside, and it only takes a strong wind. We are just thankful the Lord prevented it from falling on our house. But we must not be concerned only for our safety. Many trees have fallen in this area, and many folks are flooded out of their homes."

Anxiously I interjected, "But Daddy, can't we go out now and see if Elaine is alive?"

"No, we must be patient," he warned. "The winds are too strong yet to venture out. Do you remember that Elaine's house was built over part of a large tree trunk? No doubt when the tree was uprooted, it simply lifted the small house right off its foundation."

Marian Roth called to relieve Mother's mind about Kathryn. She would be staying at Roths until the storm was over. Mother was not anxious about her, as she usually stopped by with Marian on the way home from school to chat and drink lemonade. Marian also reported that the Forests were unhurt and were patiently waiting for the storm to pass so they could make some effort to collect some of their belongings which were blown all over the neighborhood.

The winds' velocity lessened a bit and we decided to prepare for bed. Daddy reminded us that God controlled the winds and He would take care of us.

The area was a major disaster, especially in some nearby towns that were hit worse than we were. The next several days emergency crews were working busily everywhere. The hurricane tragically destroyed 1,836 lives, injured at least as many and caused thousands of dollars in property damages as it made its devastating path along the coast.

Hospitals and mortuaries were overflowing; garages and stores, schools and other places were quickly set up to accommodate the influx of bodies, both injured and dead. Many were homeless, hungry and desolate. All persons who were able became a part of the emergency crew, working long hours without food or rest. Daddy and the boys did their part to alleviate the suffering and help with the cleanup.

The stench of death was noticeable in our town, but the most heartrending of all were the young children that perished. They were the innocent victims of the storm.

I never quite recovered from that traumatic experience. An inner anxiety gripped me whenever we had heavy storms and high winds thereafter. My parents made every possible effort to help me overcome my fear. There were times I could successfully conceal my anxiety, appearing outwardly calm, but inside the storm was raging with greater velocity than the natural one outside.

Chapter 9

Remembering Our Roots

September swept in with her rain cape on, and we needed one too. On one particular Thursday night after supper, the family had congregated on the back porch. It had just rained, and the air was pleasantly cool. Daddy and Mother were seated side by side on the porch swing. Little Elizabeth was making designs in the sand as she wiggled and moved her dainty feet. Kathryn was absorbed in a magazine she could barely read in the falling shades of night. Bill was propped lazily against the pillars which supported the porch, whistling softly to himself. Bob and Myles had just returned from a walk. I had chosen to sit on the sun-warmed third step close enough that I could hear all that was said.

"Well, the Ku Klux Klan are at it again!" exclaimed Bob, while he draped himself over the edge of the porch.

Myles was thoughtful and silent as he giant-stepped up beside Bob and sat down.

Eyeing him, I wondered, "What's he so concerned about?"

"Hey, where have you two guys been? I looked all over for you." Bill asked somewhat resentfully.

"Ah, we just took a walk," Myles answered.

"A walk! It must have been a secret one, and you sure didn't want me!" retorted Bill.

"Matter of fact, we had some important business to discuss . . . " Bob began, when Bill interrupted him sarcastically.

"Yeah, I know, you didn't need my advice!"

Daddy's "Noah!" just once was enough.

We waited for the air to clear so Bob could continue his thoughts.

"Myles and I would like to travel. I have already made arrangements to go west before December, as you know. I heard from McFarlow today, and he says he can use me on his ranch. I'm getting anxious to go. I always wanted to see the

38

West like you did, Dad."

"But where does Myles fit into all this?" Mother inquired.

Little Elizabeth had been aware of what was said. Quickly she left her sand pile and scampered over to Bob, plopping herself on his tummy. Leaning up to his face, she begged, "Please, may I go, too?"

"No," he whispered in her ear as he gave her a bear hug and a kiss. Then he gently added, "Maybe when you grow up to be a big girl."

The corners of her mouth dropped, but she said nothing.

Myles cleared his throat several times, which meant he was waiting to talk. Seven pairs of eyes focused on him, and he could feel the expectant stares even in the soft darkness of the night. Naturally shy, all this attention no doubt made him blush with embarrassment.

He slowly commented, "I've thought about this for a long time, and I have saved my money. I have over five hundred dollars. This is enough to cover my expenses in case I cannot find a job and want to return. I'll stay a couple of weeks with Cousin Paul. He feels certain about a job for me."

We occasionally received the newspaper from Pennsylvania, and Myles would often scan the employment columns.

Mother's blue eyes were moist as she listened. I saw the expression of longing—almost sadness. Was it because the boys were leaving us, or because she was too overcome with homesickness?

We had planned earlier to go swimming, but it was after nine before we left the back porch. Our two older brothers were the center of our thoughts and conversation that night as we endlessly peppered them with questions.

Kathryn and I finally tackled the supper dishes. She always washed, and I dried them. Reaching for the last dish, I said, "What a small family we'll have when they are gone. Of course, that means less dishes."

She nodded silently in agreement, then gave her dish cloth a quick twist, squirting water around and on me before she hung it up.

"Hey! That hit me in the eye," I chided her.

39

This time there was no ensuing squabble from that stinging squirt. Our minds were still churning over the startling announcements made by our brothers. In no time at all we were in bed lying side by side.

"Goodnight, Kathryn, I'll see you in Pennsylvania," I whispered with a snicker. Unable to sleep, I watched the bright white-ice moon sharpen her fine features as the blades of light cut into the dark shadows of our room. How beautiful she was—like a Dresden china doll with her high brow slightly hidden under a cloud of silken blond hair. "How can she sleep on a night like this?" I thought.

Carefully I moved out of the bed toward the nearby window. It was midnight; the Packing House whistle told me so as its clear notes were heard across the town.

Bathed in the moon's white shine, the earth acquired a virgin's gown. The dew painted jewels on thorn-tipped cactus plants, palmetto shafts and pine needles. All of nature seemed to capture the moonbeams, transforming their sharpness into a silvery softness.

Breathing deeply, I exhaled with pure delight! Sweet was the scent of orange blossoms spraying their fragrance through the night air, a perfect night for a walk.

A faint rustle made me turn from my fantasies. Then I heard it again. I tiptoed across the room, then paused at the doorway. At the end of the hall the bathroom door stood wide open. Like a silhouette in an over-exposed negative, Myles stood in his pajamas. His chin was resting in his hands and, lost in thought, he quietly gazed out of the window.

My "Pss-s-t" interrupted his reverie and he turned. I whispered, "Are you all right, or are you sick or something?" Only later in years did I learn that this was his "hiding place," where a man could go when he had to weep, or think things through.

My concerns were ignored as he growled, "Go back to bed."

Rebuffed by his reply, I returned to bed. "Oh, I guess I won't miss him so much after all. Besides, Bill will still be home," and with that I fell asleep.

Mother's announcement at the breakfast table was like a

bombshell. Things seemed to take their normal course until we started to leave the table. It was just like Mother to do it this way. Her eyes were a giveaway. She had a secret and was willing to share it!

"Daddy and I have a surprise for you," she began. "We feel you all should learn to know your relatives before you are fully grown."

Letters and pictures were the only means we had to become acquainted with our kinfolk. So our parents decided that the whole family would return to Pennsylvania for a few months.

"Daddy and I will both work while we are there and this will help with expenses. Perhaps Bob will reconsider his trip west and go along with us?"

Bob said he had to think about it first.

"But Mother, why didn't you tell us before? When will we be going up north? Will we see honest-to-goodness snow? Real snow?" Catching a quick breath, I burst forth again. "Will we go to school up there? If it's before Christmas, I'll have to give up all my parts in the school and Sunday school play programs. I just can't wait till I can tell Elizabeth. Is she still sleeping?"

"Mae, if you quiet down long enough, I'll answer some of your questions." Mother wedged her sentence between my endless line of chatter.

Glancing at Kathryn, I detected a faint rejection to all this wonderful news. "Hey, Kit, we will be late for school," I yelled, as I tore out the door. She followed only a few steps behind me down Pine Street. When she caught up with me I asked "Don't you really want to go to Pennsylvania? You're the one who said you dreamed of meeting 'the man in your life' in Pennsylvania. Doesn't the Leighty family live up there? After six years it's about time we return, or nobody will remember us anymore!"

In a superior tone she calmly stated, "I'm as excited as you are to go North. But what about Charles? I'm just learning to know him—what if Dorothy moves into my place while I'm gone!"

In a flash, I came back with words wiser than my years. "If he really fell in love with you, he won't drop you that easily."

"Hummm" was her only reply.

As we parted in front of the large school, we went directly to our respective rooms for morning devotions which always preceded our school work. Later, when my teacher in geography asked which state we would like to study about that month, I was not slow to volunteer an answer, "Pennsylvania."

I was delighted to hear her ask, "Why did you choose Pennsylvania, Mae?"

Promptly with some pride I answered, "Because that's where I have my roots," quoting Dad's remark from last night.

I was a bit embarrassed when she remarked, "Oh, so you are a Pennsylvania Dutch girl?"

Dauntlessly I replied, "Yes, and I'm proud of it!" Not really knowing why I was so proud, I decided then and there I would find out what Pennsylvania had that made it so wonderful to our family.

Chapter 10

Pennsylvania Hospitality

Warm days moved into cooler ones, and before Thanksgiving we were packing to go north. At last November eighteenth arrived. It was quite a commotion until all of us were packed in the two cars. A big trunk rested on the rear bumper of the Maxwell, plus a small cupboard on the one side. This cage-like thing was loaded so tightly that it made the car look like it was tipped backwards to the degree that it might tilt over. But by the time the inside of the car was packed and we were all seated in it, the car resumed a normal level.

Since Bob decided to join us, he led the way in his little navy coupé. We were allowed to take turns riding with him. Myles had decided to remain longer in Pennsylvania than we had planned, so he had more suitcases. It was no time to think how much I would miss him if he stayed. It was all I could do to restrain myself from bursting with excitement and eager anticipation.

The colder weather proved an aid to hurry us along. We stopped about nine o'clock at night and found a lodging place. Arising early the next day we ate cold cereal which we had packed in the cupboard on the side of the car. The carton of milk was still usable and was soon emptied.

By noon our stomachs were growling audibly again; so we stopped along the roadside. Canned heat provided the means to warm baked beans which were served with peanut butter sandwiches. The cannister of oatmeal and sugar cookies diminished quickly. With the food supply so low, we all knew we must arrive at Aunt Sybilla's soon or else we would have to buy food, which Daddy had not planned on doing. So the men kept a heavy foot on the pedal, and we did not linger long to do any sightseeing.

It took three days and two nights to arrive in Pennsylvania. Aunt "Billy" was anxiously waiting for us as we pulled up in front of her large two-story frame house. Her concern was precipitated by our late arrival, nevertheless she graciously kept a hot meal in the oven: roast beef, baked potatoes, peas, homemade bread, and three whole apple pies. What a treat for us! After washing a bit, we hurried to the loaded table. During the meal I glanced every now and then at our parents. Mother had carefully instructed us on how we were to behave. One rule was to say "no, thank you" when offered the second helping. "Remember, there're eight of us, and we don't want to eat Aunt Billy out of house and home." I peeked at Bill, and he was munching on his third piece of bread! I tried to give him a rebuking look, but he paid no heed to me.

Mother and Daddy were still talking about our trip, and we children were politely waiting to be excused. However, weary and sleepy as we were, none of us were eager to retire.

Aunt Billy resembled Mother somewhat, at least one could identify them as sisters. But her personality lacked the quiet dignity Mother carried. Also, she was a wee bit more slender. Her chestnut colored hair was so curly it was difficult for her to arrange it neatly under her white prayer veil. This two-piece prayer cap covered her ears and was secured to her head by two black, narrow ribbons which tied under her chin. Her eyes were a light blue and often twinkled with laughter. We all loved her, and she accepted all eight of us — baggage and all.

Those weeks in her home were memorable ones. I can still smell the damp arid odor which was so noticeable in many old houses where homemade soap was used, where large cellars were stacked with shelves of canned fruit, vegetables and meats, and where coal bins were piled high with their bluish black pebbles. What a fascinating place to explore! One exciting, unfamiliar feature which we discovered was a closet-like place where a pile of shelves moved from the cellar to the kitchen. Food, apple cider, milk and various other items were placed on these shelves and, with a little pressure, were slowly lowered or raised accordingly. Aunt Billy called it a dumb waiter.

Auntie had a generous heart and a spontaneous sense of humor, although tears flooded her eyes as she recalled her husband's unexpected death. Her two sons were fourteen and seventeen years old. Kathryn whispered to me that it was too

44

bad we were cousins. But a very close friendship did develop among us. Hiram was a handsome boy with his dark curly hair, and he loved to tease and flirt with Kathryn.

Two weeks passed all too quickly, and we still were unable to find a house to rent on short terms. The realtors were not interested in short-term renters.

The next place we were cordially invited to visit was Aunt Maria's. She had even a larger house than Aunt Billy's, but she had more family at home: her oldest son and his wife, three single children (two adults, and one teenager), also her husband, Uncle Harry. He was a rather picturesque person, muscular and tall. His prominent nose was not too noticeable because of a full white beard which extended below his breast bone. His kind eyes and generous heart made him a lifelong friend to our family.

Aunt Maria also wore a large white cap. But her straight dark hair, neatly knotted, did not need to be tied on with little black ribbons under her chin. Unlike Aunt Billy, she did not favor the rest of her sisters. Beneath her long aproned dress was an angular figure. Her small gray eyes were lined, and she appeared older than her years. Many mothers those days had protruding stomachs. Tight undergarments were not too popular and often hindered their movements. Aunt Maria believed in being "chust as she vass," which meant she could be pregnant, and no one noticed at least for the first six months.

She loved Mother and accepted what she called our "high-falutin' manners" as unnecessary. To say "pardon me" for a re-sounding burp was silly to her. Starches and pastries were her specialties, and everyone was either fat or overweight. Teasingly we were called "skinny little Florida Crackers."

This change in diet made us susceptible to colds. Even with thick feathertick comforters we were not able to keep warm. Florida's climate had thinned our blood. Pennsylvania's spring temperatures ranging from thirty to forty degrees seemed freezing to us. I recall heated bricks being placed in our beds. The only room that had any heat was the bedroom that had a stovepipe coming up through it from the potbellied stove in the living room. But unfortunately we did not occupy this room during our stay at Aunt Maria's.

45

Chapter 11

Ghosts and Chamber Pots

Finally Daddy found a temporary home for us to occupy until we would return to Florida. He also found a short-term maintenance job. Mother felt it was necessary for her to work, too, so she was employed at a sewing factory not too far from our home.

This house, if one could call it that, was previously unoccupied because of its aged and neglected condition. Actually, it was a squatty log cabin — perhaps more than 150 years old. The logs on the outside were exactly like the log cabins of early American style. The steps were hollowed with wear. Low ceiling and concave floors creaked and groaned when a heavy person walked through the rooms.

An old organ in the parlor was moved into the shadowy hall because the rotting planks threatened to collapse under its weight. Antique as it was, it conveyed a dignity which spoke of better days.

There were no closets in the rooms upstairs. Naked electric bulbs staggered from cracked ceilings; raw wires were dangerously exposed. Plaster and paper had long since refused to stay put. The three bedrooms each had a wire stretched across one corner. No doubt these served as closets. Two had straggly cloths hanging on the wires; likely they served as covers for the garments which were hung there.

It was obvious that this old house had been unoccupied for some time. One of our neighbors hinted about ghosts! Rodents and insects resented our intrusion and moved about in almost a defiant manner. Thousand-leggers gave me no end of agitation! The small, deep-set windows allowed a scarce amount of fresh air. Some locked their jaws on the decaying sills. Others we coaxed open with a crow bar, but only a man's strong arm could close them.

Mother attended public sales to purchase necessary articles

to furnish our crude home. Even with all our efforts the rooms were hardly cheerful. But we quickly adjusted . . . except for one article which certainly was necessary—a chamber pot! Some pots came with a set: a china pitcher, a deep basin and a soap dish. All had dainty flowers painted on them. Some included cameos of lovely ladies with roses. These potties were more politely silent when the user learned how to place himself on them. The metal pots were something else. To have no bathroom was indeed a chilling experience by day and a noisy, embarrassing one at night. I'm not sure how the men's feet appeared after their bath, as only small feet would fit into the basins we had. If I was a blue baby when I was born, I must have been a purple child after a bath on a chilly morn!

But we were so enthralled with all these new experiences that inconveniences were not too bad, especially if one accepted the situation as a temporary thing. We thus adopted our weird little log house, ghosts and all, as our temporary home.

The cellar was one to be remembered. It was endowed with two arch-like divisions. It was a fearsome thing to be down there when others were treading across the floor above. Since the house was condemned for safety purposes, we dreaded going downstairs for any reason. Dad bought bags of potatoes and apples and they were placed in the cellar. Every conceivable excuse could be invented to escape a trip to the cellar.

On work days Kathryn automatically assumed the responsibility of the house and minding us three siblings. She did this willingly. She provided many hours of exciting entertainment, for from her imagination came a constant flow of stories. The ghost stories were so real that Elizabeth and I were afraid to move away from her side. While pumping air into the wheezing old organ, she could conjure up all the necessary sounds to accompany her chilling tales of wandering spirits and rattling bones with clanging chains.

Sometimes all four of us decided to sneak pennies from Mother's purse to buy peanut-bolsters. Guilty and ashamed, we would eventually confess to Mother what we had done. Later we learned that she purposefully placed her purse with its five cents or eight cents where we could help ourselves. How we enjoyed those one-cent peanut-bolsters!

Myles enjoyed and prospered in his work as a store clerk. Being a private sort of person, making friends was difficult, and he grew lonely for his social life in Florida. Near the end of our stay in Pennsylvania, he decided to return with us.

By this time Bob was well established as a bellhop in a luxurious hotel, a vacationing spot in the Catskill Mountains. He was an outgoing person and was soon caught up in the social life which this resort was noted for. It was not long before his lifestyle changed. He became an excellent partner on the dance floor and a convivial person at the bar. He was easily involved in the meaningless pleasures of the rich. This continued for a year.

Our parents were troubled and concerned as his letters revealed his activities and experiences. Kathryn and I were fascinated by his wild escapades. Once he shared a "hot" story with us concerning an evening when he was serving at a banquet. That night he served a select group of nobility. As he began serving the soup, a backless gowned lady accidentally tipped his tray, and over her bare back ran the steaming soup! This incident terminated his service as a waiter.

I am sure Mother's tearful prayers brought about a change in Bob's future. We received a telegram from him reporting he was on his way to Wyoming to work on a large ranch. All of us at home were disappointed, as we had anticipated a promised visit. The next airmail letter announced that he found ranch life quite exciting and would remain out there for at least six months. Delightful was the taste of travel and adventure, and he was not ready to settle down.

Chapter 12

Sand in Our Shoes Again

Three months, like flashing scenes on a screen, were gone. We could not believe it was time to return to Florida again. By the end of February all our luggage was packed and piled outside in front of the log cabin we had occupied. We waited eagerly for Daddy to drive our new car up to the curb. The old Maxwell had been turned in, and we now owned a second-hand blue Ford.

With much oh'ing and ah'ing we settled back to enjoy this trip in the larger vehicle. Our emotions were mixed as we headed toward the state highway. Several miles later I discovered to my surprise a small hidden pocket in the lining of the car door. I cautiously slipped my hand into it, and behold, it yielded a treasure—two dimes and a nickel, one glove, and some chewing gum. No one seemed to notice my discovery so I replaced the articles. I wrestled with the desire to claim it all for myself and keep it a secret. But as evening came on, I could not contain my secret any longer.

I leaned forward and whispered in Daddy's ear, "I found some money in a pocket in the door; must I send it back?"

I was sure he would say "yes" and I would have to relinquish my treasure. But to my amazement he calmly whispered back, "No, keep it. They simply didn't care enough to check the pockets."

I sighed with relief and promptly promised myself some further searching.

After four days of wearisome travel, we were eager to return to our home in Florida. It was considerably warmer when we arrived in Sebring. Wafting through the balmy air came all the familiar odors—the ambrosial sweetness from the citrus blossoms, the hemmed sand bars blanket-stitched with seaweed, fish skeletons and other debris. The gentle breasts of the blue lakes heaved gracefully as each breath waved into the

49

shore. We would pause for a better view of such breathtaking landscapes.

We tarried at the St. Augustine Fort, which proved an interesting tour. This visit provided a lengthy supply of gory stories to conjure up and share. Kathryn could capture anyone's attention with her imagination.

Although we loved Pennsylvania and hoped someday to live there permanently, nevertheless we were looking forward to moving back into the life we were most adapted to.

We enjoyed the daily swims and the more relaxed way people lived in the South. All of us children were healthy, and Daddy's restored health was a big factor for staying there.

The neighbors greeted us with a warm welcome, and we shared countless experiences with them. Our daily activities seemed less burdensome. Mother often sang while she worked. In this pleasant mild climate, Daddy barely coughed at all.

Chapter 13

Struggles With Conscience

In my sixth year at school, we were encouraged to participate in plays, gym performances and folk dancing. All this really appealed to me, for I simply loved acting.

In the back of our new home was a large park. Much of the land was a sand yard. All kinds of apparatus on which to perform were placed at various areas — seesaws, ladders, swings, merry-go-rounds and also sliding boards of various sizes. Tall pine trees, some huddled together and others in singles, gave a reasonable amount of shade. To the far left was an open auditorium. Although it opened on all sides except one, there were heavy linen-like curtains rolled and fastened at the tops. During the wet season the curtain gave a measure of protection to the audience. The large auditorium was called a Chautauqua house. Its large stage was frequently utilized and drew large crowds of theater-hungry people. Many performers were well known and provided excellent entertainment.

This was not the kind of entertainment our parents desired for their children. True, we heard forbidden words, and the acting was called immoral and ungodly. But we also learned to appreciate true art from highly gifted people in the world of music, dancing and acting. Numerous times I would sneak over into the park, stand in the rear and watch with the greatest fascination. I longed secretly to be an actress, to dance so gracefully, to try to express all the longings and wild emotions I had in my heart.

When I was asked to participate in a folk dance performance in school which would climax our May Day celebration, I was thrilled. I practiced tirelessly after school to perfect my steps and motions. I deceptively described this performance as a "gymnastic display" to my parents. Mother was not enthusiastic, but remained silent about the whole program.

Sister Kitty was chosen as an attendant to the May Day

Queen. Her parts did not require dancing but graceful movements as the attendants entwined pastel ribbons about the May Pole, thus forming shades and patterns; all ending wth a colorful canopy for the queen. The event took place on the Circle which was in the center of town—a large, park-like area shaped like a wheel.

Finally May Day arrived, the first Saturday of the month. I was to wear a short, white, fluffy dress and white shoes and socks. Mother taught us never to expose our bodies unnecessarily. All the girls wore shorter dresses than I and they always wore their socks several inches below their knees. When I got to school, I would roll mine down, then replace them on the way home. I knew this was deceitful, but it was so important to me to be like all my friends. This also included belt tightening so my dresses would look shorter.

At any rate, this May Day morning I awakened early. The program started at two o'clock, but we had to be there at twelve-thirty for a rehearsal practice. I knew I had to help with the Saturday chores, which I willingly did. The laundry had to be done not only for us, but for several families. I would dutifully help to push the handle which churned the wash. In those days this was a fairly modern washing machine. We all took turns. Mother turned out snow white sheets and table linens. Her special pride was starched shirts returned with a "store-bought" look.

This Saturday morning Dad had just finished pouring buckets of boiling water into the huge rinsing tub. Mother always warned us to keep a respectful distance from these tubs. I was barefooted, and for some silly reason I wanted to test the temperature by scarcely touching the surface with my toe, just to see if I could stand such heat. My other foot supporting all my weight tilted accidentally, and somehow I lost my balance. Before I knew what happened, my left leg rested in the boiling water. Myles was taking his turn at pushing the washer handle, and he quickly came to my aid. As I screamed with pain, he picked me up and called Mother who was approaching the kitchen door with a basket of soiled clothes. She opened the door and anxiously waited for me to become coherent. Myles gently set me down on the couch in the kitchen. I was sobbing pitifully while Mother tried to elevate my scalded limb. She promptly made a plaster of baking soda and water and gently applied it to the burned area. This painful experience concerned each member of the family. Daddy felt I should see a doctor. I begged not to be moved, and before I knew what happened, the doctor had arrived and was examining my scarlet leg. All this was such a traumatic experience. Aside from the intense physical pain, I suffered from a deeper kind of injury, as I realized, "I'll miss the May Day performance!"

And miss it I did! It took hours for the severe pain to lessen. Huge blisters developed which the doctor had to open. Plaster upon plaster was applied.

Sensitive to my conscience, I wondered if this was God's way of dealing with my deceitful nature.

As Kitty appeared in her long flowing gown in which she would join the rest of the attendants on the Circle, I was crushed with longing and despair. How could such a disappointing thing happen to me! "Oh, Mother," I cried, "couldn't Daddy drive me up to the Circle and I could stay in the car and watch?"

With tender sympathy she answered, "No, dear, the doctor says you have a temperature, and it will mean you will have to stay in bed at least a week."

All the get-well cards I received did not pour balm on my disappointed spirit. I had lifelong scars to remind me. But in spite of this my determined longings to act and, yes, to dance, were not quelled. Later I took leading parts in plays in Sunday school and public school and earned favorable comments and praise.

Once I was requested to do the Charleston in the Saturday night musical program down at the band shell. This also was an entertainment center which totally involved hometown talents. I was thrilled to try for a place of honor with a promise to repeat the performance. But my parents were quick to refuse permission to compete for such a worldly thing. Again, I was disappointed but not surprised. I knew only too well how conservative they were.

Mother and Dad did, however, allow me to take various

parts in plays portraying religious characters. But secretly I had made up my mind — someday I would learn to become a real actress.

Sometimes when Mother would catch me dancing to the music of our old victrola, she would have a sad expression on her face and gently inquire, "Is that what you want to be doing when Jesus comes for us?"

This same question was often applied at times of misconduct, or times when I would become unreasonably angry. I can well remember how angry I became over anything that appeared unfair or unjust.

There was a time when Bill was implicated along with a number of school mates in a mischievous episode. The professor of our school gave each of the boys a severe beating for their bad behavior. Although Bill was with the group, he did not participate in the mischief. The boys discovered a way to peep into the window of the local mortuary. They piled up orange crates high enough to stand on, enabling them to view the corpses as they were being embalmed. Bill was fearful of being caught and refused to take his turn to peep. Later, when our parents learned what happened and witnessed the bluish red welts on Bill's thighs and legs, they were really upset. True, the fellows were in the wrong, but they all claimed Bill had taken no part in the act. Yet, of all the boys his punishment seemed the most severe.

The professor received letters from parents protesting and reproving him, even threatening him for administering such severe punishment. From that time on, I hated that professor! I cried quietly for Bill's wounds. In the school corridor one morning, discussing the incident with my friends, I said, "He better never lay a hand on me. If he does, I'll kick and scratch him!" To my horror there he was, walking right behind us! Admittedly, I was frightened; my heart was in my throat. As he passed us I gave his back the most angry and defiant stare I could muster. If he heard me, he paid no attention. But my anger burned, and I again burst out, "I just dare him!"

In such excited states my heart played a wild tattoo in my breast, and I trembled. When I was calmed down, I suffered from guilt and fear, wondering if I could have died in such a fit of rage. Always I had been reminded to refrain from such spells of ill will. Mother thought I behaved disgracefully when I became angry. Certainly I was not acceptable to God with so much hate in my heart.

Being so sensitive, I doubted if God could accept me, and I was frequently given to dark forebodings concerning this matter.

My spiritual training was like a school of learning. I know now that I was blessed with God-fearing parents who lived what they taught. Our daily family devotions were a must. My Sunday school teachers were dedicated. But the most worthwhile lessons were "caught" rather than taught. Moral and spiritual convictions were graven on my character.

Slang was not permitted in our home. No guest was welcome who smoked, drank or indulged in worldly appetites. Sex was a forbidden subject, so we siblings all learned in our own way what we really wanted to know about it. Our friends were not inhibited and shared their sexual knowledge whenever they could find a listening ear.

Kathryn secretly bought or borrowed *True Story* magazines. She was a true romanticist. She would hide these magazines under her mattress, providing an easy way for me to help myself, which I freely did. Although they were not that exciting to me, I begged for all the free coupons they offered and had the mailman deliver all kinds of creams, powders and what-have-you. My collection of booklets and samples did not meet Mother's approval although she did not prevent my sending for them.

When Kathryn was sixteen, Mother gave her a special personal book to read on sex, love and marriage. My curiosity got the best of me and I managed to read her private book also. Kathryn did not seem to mind my invasion on her privacy. She shared countless initmate and personal thoughts with me. I mostly listened, only asking questions when I did not understand.

By the age of twelve I was interested in boys. I had several boyfriends, one of whom was five years older than I. His older brother was a friend to Kathryn, too. He would come around dusk time and persuade me to get on the bar that joined the seat and the handle bars on his bike and away we would go. These rides were fun and innocent enough for the first few weeks. Then followed some deceptive liberties which made me very uneasy. He persuaded me that to be a real "girl friend" one must experiment to learn what one must *not* do. These "experiences" would help me to grow up. After these devious actions, he would reward me and warn me not to tell anyone. I got fed up with his disgusting "love making" and refused to meet him again. This familiarity left a deep emotional wound that took years to heal. I exaggerated the incident and brooded over it until it became insurmountable. I secretly hated and distrusted men for a long time.

Mother and others noticed my sad and depressed countenance. She encouraged me to talk and share my thoughts with her. Never could I have imagined sharing such an experience with her! My lovely Mother, what would she think of me! Besides, the young man was the son of a good friend of hers.

I was overwhelmed with guilt and had no one to turn to. Sometimes I would hide behind a large hibiscus bush, forlorn and afraid. I hugged my knees close and hid my face, weeping my heart out. How despicable I must be to God!

Chapter 14

Revival and Rebellion

Two blocks from the center of town nestled our neat little white church. Its verdant carpet surrounded all sides, broken only by white ribbon sidewalks. It was a five minute walk from our home and just one and a half blocks from the lake. This little worship center entertained some of the greatest and godliest men in the faith. Since Sebring was a tourist town, we were privileged to hear many guest speakers. Families met here not only to worship, but to eat, study and play together. We opened our hearts and minds to each other, thus cementing lifelong friendships.

Revival meetings, like the seasons, came annually spring and fall. Young people were motivated by the stirring "invitations" given; many "went forward" to become church members, thereby "insuring" their souls for eternal life. Each of my brothers and Kathryn "went forward" during these evangelistic thrusts. It was a beautiful sight to witness these young people robed in long white gowns as they walked to the lakeside where a baptismal service was reverently performed.

Church life was woven into the very warp and woof of my being. God had to be in everything. No happening or event occurred without knowing God was in it somewhere. Our parents never entertained the thought of being absent from any church service. Sickness was the only exception made. Sometimes this faithful attendance became a hardship to us children, especially around exam time at school. On the other hand, this training proved to be a stabilizing factor in our mental and emotional development. Consciously or unconsciously we were absorbing the Word.

In the fall of 1929, our own Pastor Paul Forest preached the remaining four nights of the evangelistic meetings. The guest evangelist was called away on an emergency. Since Pastor Forest's daughter Elaine was my friend, I was often influenced by her ideas and actions. She confided that her daddy thought it was time we make up our minds to join the church. From time to time over revival periods, my mother would tactfully approach the subject, reminding me that I was not prepared to die or meet the Lord if He should suddenly come! I wearied of hearing this and made myself scarce as soon as I could politely do so.

But now Elaine had persuaded our group of girls that this was the time "to go forward." Milly, the most intelligent of us five, took it seriously. She said, "Hell's an awful place to be in forever. Let's all go forward together and be saved. I'll lead the way."

I dreaded the thought of going forward, but since everyone else was going I decided to submit to their plans.

Daddy always sat up on the second pew from the front because he was hard-of-hearing. He had a beautiful tenor voice and enjoyed singing "heartily as unto the Lord," as he would say. When he would sing I would press my ear against his side and feel all the vibrations as he hit the deep notes. Somehow it gave me a real sense of joy and comfort. It made me feel pious and good inside.

Sitting with Daddy allowed us a whole pew to ourselves. Rarely did anyone share our pew since it was so far front. We had a special privilege — a close view of the minister and some deacons.

Since I liked to draw, Daddy always carried a notebook and a pencil which he would remove from his vest pocket and hand to me after the offering. Drawing the profiles around me was interesting. Daddy said I caught a real resemblance of the brethren. This pastime kept me awake.

Daddy was rather surprised this one Sunday night when all four of my girl friends came up and sat in our pew. The girls were unusually serious that night and listened to every word Brother Forest said. I leaned against Daddy for a while and grew drowsy. Then I started passing notes, but none were returned. Becoming bored, I laid my head against Dad's shoulder and fell asleep.

Suddenly, I felt someone shake my arm and whisper, "Mae, get up; it's time to go forward." I had difficulty getting my eyes to open. I heard again in a louder whisper, "Mae, its' time to go forward!"

The plaintive strains of "Just As I Am" was imploring sinners to come. Oh, yes, I had promised I would go forward with the girls. "Wretched and blind . . . ". Somehow I made my way out of the pew and stood alongside the other four girls. With the last strains of "I come, I come," I was fully aware of where I was. Three of the girls were crying. Elaine sniffed a time or two, but I was planning the quickest way to get out of the church. As soon as Pastor Forest shook our hands and invited the audience to greet these fine saved souls, I hastily made my exit through the side door. I could not tolerate all that kissing and handshaking. I ran all the way home and waited in silence for the family to return. My thoughts were noisy as they jostled around with questions.

Now I was "saved," they said, and I was supposed to be different. I did not feel as holy as my friends appeared to feel. Nor was it either a sad or a joyous experience for me. What was wrong? I wondered.

When my parents returned, Dad reproved me with, "Why did you run out of the church before anyone could greet you?" Mother came over and kissed me; her cheeks were wet with tears. She warmly caressed me and softly added, "I am so glad you have given your heart to Jesus tonight." Her gentle love melted my rebellious spirit, and I began to wonder why I felt so unmoved when everyone else thought it was such a soul-cleansing experience.

Finally I burst out and said, "I just don't like all that kissing and fuss they make over you when you join the church!" Daddy thought it was a poor testimony for one who just accepted Christ.

Our baptismal service was held the following Sunday afternoon. The sun had transformed the lake into a shimmering pane of glass. It was a peaceful scene as each of us were led into the water. Our mothers wept, and others watched in reverent silence. We were immersed three times forward under the water, in the name of the Father, Son and Holy Spirit. This was an outward testimony that we died with Christ and were risen in newness of life in Him.

59

This meant we were now members of the church and could take communion. Our church had "closed" communion: for members only. This included a Love Feast followed by the Holy Communion service. We began with the ordinance of feet washing, and we exchanged a kiss of fellowship. Then followed a meal consisting of stewed lamb and a bread soup. We were served small portions of meat, bread and butter. After the meal came the Holy Communion service, partaking of the sacraments of the bread and the wine. In our church there was one cup to be shared by all the women, and one cup for all the men. In spite of such an unsanitary custom, one never learned of transmitted diseases.

That night in bed, lying beside Kathryn, I whispered, "How did you feel when you went up to the altar?"

Waiting a moment to recall her experiences, she softly answered, "So much better, because I had become a Christian."

"But Kathryn, you are the same person you always were. Besides, I just can't stand all that kissing stuff! Anyway, I never wore jewelry and makeup like you did. So what is there to give up except socks?" And heatedly I added, "I'll always wear socks, even if old Annie does tell me it's a sin!"

Dear, godly Annie, who lived across the way from us, would sometimes hint to Mother that we were a pretty worldly family—we children were. Many were the reproofs Mother patiently endured as Annie recounted all our worldly sins and misdeeds. We siblings sometimes resented Annie's interferences. But Mother accepted Annie's fallacious ways and remained a good friend to her.

If that gentle, loving Holy Spirit had been in my heart that Sunday night, I scarcely knew it and surely could not witness to any change in my life.

Chapter 15

The North in Our Blood

In his senior year of high school, Myles was unsettled. Once again he decided he was going north — this time to stay. Not waiting to graduate, he left Sebring in early March to travel by train to Pennsylvania. Employment was plentiful in Pennsylvania, and immediately he became a clerk in a Thom McAn Shoe Store. He enrolled in several night courses. Soon he was promoted to manager of the store.

His letters conveyed touches of homesickness, but mostly we read about a maturing young man who could handle responsibility and was involved in church work. At first, he jokingly referred to the girl he was dating, but later we learned he was serious about her.

Since Robert returned to Pennsylvania and was rooming in Lancaster, the brothers saw much of one another. Myles and Robert would frequently double-date, although at that time Robert was not serious about romantic involvements.

Kathryn, too, was restless and bored in school. She longed to be back in Pennsylvania. She dropped out of her classes in the tenth grade and found employment with a wealthy family who needed a nursemaid for their two young children.

Kathryn and Bill were in the same age group of young people. They had a close relationship and shared their romantic experiences and were never known to betray the other's confidences. Even with this relationship, Bill missed his brothers and wished to be in Pennsylvania with them.

When Kathryn was home, she would try to coax Mother and Dad to return to Pennsylvania. Imitating her, I began a crusade "back to Pennsylvania where everything is better!" At first it amused our parents, but as it continued they began to heed the hints. One night they called us in for a family council meeting. They tactfully reminded us that we would have no place to live if we were to make such a move. We owned a

61

home in Florida but no property in Pennsylvania. Nor could we sponge on the relatives.

"No," Daddy reasoned, "such a move would have to be planned well ahead of time."

Advantageous as the years were in Florida, they were running thin. We longed for our relatives and the beautiful changing seasons. Then, too, Pennsylvania's economic levels were higher. One could earn higher wages there than in the South doing the average man's labor.

Daddy reluctantly decided he would pull up stakes. Soliciting the help of the boys in Pennsylvania, a house was found that could be available for us by the time we were ready to move.

We children were thrilled over this permanent move. We were instructed by our parents, however, that there would be some drastic changes. The church discipline and the form of dress was much more conservative. That meant that we girls must let our hair grow long and wear it up in a bun with a prayer veil to cover our hair. Although Mother always wore one, I could never imagine my sisters or myself wearing our hair in the same style. My proud heart had a rebellious struggle, and I was sure I would figure out some way to escape this church discipline.

There were the school changes to adjust to as well as differences in educational levels. But in spite of all these adjustments, we were eager to return to Pennsylvania.

Chapter 16

Angels in Trouble

Our family left Florida May 2, 1931, for the last time, but most of us did return for visits in later years. Saying goodbye was a tearful experience for all of us. We had many dear friends and a close affiliation with our dear little Sebring church.

By the third week of May, we were pretty well settled in our quaint little home on North Main Street in Manheim, Pennsylvania. Some parts of this house had been remodeled and made more convenient, such as a flush toilet placed in a dark little closet and a sink in the kitchen with running cold water. The outhouse was a usable shack, and the pump in the shanty provided an excellent place to wash vegetables and to be a makeshift bathhouse for the men folk.

The house's two potbellied stoves furnished us with ample heat in the early fall, but winter months were pretty cold. The old iron cook stove with its huge oven consumed a tremendous amount of wood and coal. Neat stacks of wood were piled high in the shanty, which was a little enclosed porch that somehow clung tenaciously to the rear of the house!

With this minimum amount of heat, we became victims of colds and accompanying fevers, Daddy and I succumbing every couple of weeks. After a bout with double pleurisy, my health never regained its normal state.

This unusual house manifested an era of German culture. Its deep window sills begged for bright geraniums and colorful potted plants. Faded wallpaper tenaciously clung to the ceilings and walls. Gold and ivory tracings of hoop-skirted ladies were waving to armed men marching off to war. The upstairs walls were skinless; other places were onion-shell thin, a mere touch and off it came. This was far too tempting for me. Besides, I figured I could redecorate my room by peeling off loose parts and creating a design with the bare spaces. Carefully I peeled away, measuring the spaces between each new design. Delighted with the results, I could hardly wait until some member of the family would come and discover my artistic ability!

I did not have to wait long. I held my breath as Mother's steps neared the door. Stepping into the room, her arms piled high with fresh laundry, she carefully deposited it on the bed. Then she straightened the covers of the bed where I had been standing and suddenly she became aware of my "art work."

The silence was broken with a gasp. "Oho-o-a-h! Mae, did you do that? Who gave you permission to remove all that paper from the walls?" Mother was angry and dismayed.

"But, Mother," I exclaimed, "I thought you would like my designs. The paper was coming off anyway!" It never occurred to me that I was defacing the walls. Had I not peeled a lifesize angel on the wall, a larger-than-life rabbit, a cat, some birds and some silhouettes of my family? And anyway, stars on the ceiling were much more attractive than rain-soaked blotches!

As she turned to go, our eyes met. They were not as angry as her voice. "Well, we will have to take this matter up with Daddy," she remarked in a perturbed voice. This meant a promise of some sort of punishment. Waiting for this discipline was worse than the discipline itself.

One day at the dinner table we were discussing a scary subject. It was about an escaped murderer. Forgetting to avoid the subject of the defaced walls, I blurted out, "I don't need to be afraid; I have a guardian angel in my room!"

Dad overheard my remark, and firmly rejected it with this weighty statement: "Yes, and that very angel may have caused us a lawsuit were it not for a tolerant landlord."

I was respectfully silent throughout the rest of the meal, although my thoughts darted hither and yon as they sketched the possible disciplines I imagined would follow such a misdeed. Evidently my parents thought the guilt and remorse I showed was punishment enough, and they never carried out the threatened discipline.

Truthfully, my art work furnished all of us siblings much entertainment and some admiration as well.

Chapter 17

A Disaster Averted

Daddy was informed about a large house on Grant Street that would be up for rent the next spring. The occupants were being evicted because the house was sadly neglected. This, of course, required time for considerable repair work. Daddy signed a contract on the promise that the house would be ours by spring. In the meantime, we were compelled to make a temporary move to a house on East High Street.

Our living room windows in this new home provided us with pictures of human interest. Across the street squatted a three-story school building. As the students poured in and out of the building, we found ourselves intrigued and entertained by their antics.

Most of our friends considered this location a pretty convenient one. For me, it proved to be a "thorn in the flesh." My physical condition worsened to the degree that I was forbidden to attend all the classes. School days were precious and I enjoyed my studies and school activities. My interest and natural ability in art gave me a measure of acceptance and approval.

I loved my art teacher, and I wanted so to do something especially nice for her. After a sleepless night pondering an appropriate gift, I resolved to buy her some flowers. Early in the morning I hurried over to the florist. Naive as I was, I did not realize that fifty cents was a meager sum for a regal bouquet of flowers. Frustrated and disappointed, I was still determined to get her something. So I bought one large white calla lily, had it wrapped, and proudly hurried back to school.

My art teacher was very special to me and I felt shy about handing her one flower. But it was the largest flower I could find for fifty cents. It had a fragrant smell, too.

I shyly walked to her desk and handed her my precious gift of love. The class had just assembled and she was preparing an introduction to modern art. My heart fluttered with affection and anticipation as she slowly tore away the tissue. The expression on her face was a "double take." I'm sure she thought it was a joke. Her large, expressive eyes flooded with merriment, but with effort she controlled her mouth and said, "Thank you, Mae, it's lovely!"

My spirits sank lower than my feet as I made my long way back to my seat! I was so tense and eager to please her. I did not hear the suppressed giggles behind me. Then I heard someone hiss, "That's a funeral lily; she must be telling Miss G. to drop dead!"

Embarrassment overwhelmed me—I shrank so small in my seat, but I could not disappear! Mechanically I placed my drawing tablet and pencils on my desk. My eyelids were clinched to dam the tears. My Adam's apple moved spasmodically, trying to erase the lumps that kept rising hard and dry in my throat.

Were my ears deceiving me now? No, my beautiful teacher was speaking these very words. "Mae has saved my day. We will use this perfect flower." Placing it in a tall, black vase (a paintbrush holder), she continued, "This will be an excellent object for a lesson on still life in contrast." Taking a scarlet velvety cloth, she gracefully draped a background. Oh's and ah's could be heard from the students as they stared in wonder at the striking creation.

My little breast heaved a deep sigh of appreciation for this understanding teacher. It was only heard by God and me.

Chapter 18

The Winter of My Discontent

As I watched the children move in and out of school every day, I thought they were the luckiest kids alive. Jealous and angry, I brooded over my lot. What would people think when they learned I had never graduated? I was positive I would never find a worthwhile job.

A doctor, a nurse, an artist, all these vocations were inviting to me. Dreams, yes, to be an actress, too. This was a hidden dream; the rest I freely talked about.

Now I was only allowed to attend two art classes a week. The upper lobe in my left lung developed a new lesion. My temperature rose a few points, which meant more rest. Although I wearied easily, I refused to become an invalid. It seemed my illness intensified my ambitions to paint and to express myself through art.

Daddy made me a fine easel. Robert bought me a large paint set, and dear Mother arranged a small room just like a studio. It was a dream come true! Countless hours were spent here where I found a large measure of happiness and fulfillment.

Mother was a farm girl, and she loved the outdoors. She would often persuade me to join her outside a she busied herself with various tasks. She would clean her vegetables in the old pump sink right beyond the back porch rather than inside where the kitchen sink made things handier.

I can still hear the harsh "scrunch," the raspy heaves of the old pump as its rusty throat was forced to regurgitate its clear cool contents. I was fascinated the way Mother's paring knife carefully nipped and crawled around her potatoes and apples. It never ended the peel till it came to the top. The long, juicy apple peel was never discarded. From these came our delicious apple preserves.

When it was cherry seeding time I always helped. Mother taught me how to detect wormy fruit by touch, and to spot pulpy fruit, too. A string bean snapped crisply when young and tender; hull peas were full shelled and had a fresh green color. Mother's lessons on culinary skills were priceless, and Daddy's long hours in the garden provided abundant supplies of food for the winter.

Mother was a frugal housekeeper and utilized everything. We were taught that wasting food was a sin. These hours of working along with her were pleasant ones. Sometimes she would become pensive and talk about the future, intimating some doubts. How would things work out after we moved? I did not understand what she meant. Perhaps she was protecting me.

Mother had an unusual appreciation for birds. How enthralled she became over a large flock of honking geese as they waveringly flew in a "V" formation across the azure sky. When the geese could no more be seen, she would sigh and say, "The summer is passed. House cleaning is right around the corner."

House cleaning was a status symbol in our community. It was both a spring and fall activity. This fall we would postpone the house-cleaning and start packing. We packed everthing we did not need and some things we did need. We would be moving soon again.

Fall emerged ostentatiously, once again displaying her artistic talents!

Beautiful Autumn

Brilliant and brazen
        were her splashes of crimson,
        gold, and purple browns.
Along with her riotous colors came
        its smells and sounds.
Dry and rattley are the twigs and trees
Arid and smokey were the piles of leaves—
        My pulse would leap
        And my pale, pale cheeks
Borrowed some rouge from her pallet.
Autumn encompassed my soul
        Sweet and beautiful autumn.
        How I love it!
If only I could write or sing—
A thousand lyrics I would bring!

Then one morning, sneaky and without warning, the thermometer changed its face! Instead of a friendly low forty degrees, it dropped into the twenties. Dark grays overcast the heavens—a forewarning of snow.

Winter crept close to us, chilling the bone, but on earth's weary breast she laid her softest eiderdown.

Christmas fluttered by like the seasonal snowflake. It was one of the happiest ones our family had together.

I had spent hours painting dishes, glasses, scarves and pictures for others. In this way I had earned a nice amount of money for Christmas gifts. Nothing delighted me more than to buy gifts with my own money.

Even though it was going into our second year that we were in Pennsylvania, there were still some adjustments to be made. I was not able to accept willingly the strict and conservative disciplines of the church. For me they were a facade. I certainly had no convictions about them.

Last year's school experience left me feeling bitter. My parents did not want to offend the church, so they asked Kathryn and me to put our hair up in a bun. (Betty did not belong to church at that time.) I hated the "old-woman look," and would take it down when I was at home. I was so upset when Mother said I would have to wear it up to school. I was the only girl in class who wore a large, two-piece prayer veil. It was made of a white net-like material and covered most of my hair. Over the prayer veil I wore a bonnet. It was larger than my veil, a wire frame covered with black, shiny material. It had a ribbon that went under the chin and hooked on the one side. This plus two long, four-inch bonnet pins held the bonnet on.

One recess time I did not go outside for that period. In the cloak rooms someone took my bonnet off the hook where I had placed it and used it as a football. When I discovered this, catching them in the act, I thought my world had come to an end.

In tears, I asked permission to go home; I simply could not face that class again. I stormed into the house holding my ruined bonnet and tearfully gave vent to my humiliation. In the meantime, a sympathetic student related the whole incident to the teacher. She admonished the class severely and ordered a discipline for all those who participated.

My parents were shocked and distressed over such inexcusable behavior. Still upset, I refused to go back to school the next day. That evening, Mother and Daddy agreed that I could wear my hair down, neatly fastened with a barrette. From that day on I wore tams to school. This emotional upheaval only helped to confuse my teenage concepts of religion.

Chapter 19

The Graybill Hotel

Spring with its capricious weather was not exactly ideal for moving. But we moved anyway, and each member of the family was pleased with the end results. There was plenty of straightening out to do. None of us complained or slacked off from our duties.

We nicknamed our home "our hotel." It was designed for a large family — and a large family we were! After the carpets were laid and the furniture placed, it took on a real homey appearance. An added benefit was a long lot in the rear with fruit trees and a raspberry hedge.

I enjoyed unpacking the china and placing it where I thought it should go. With countless clean cupboards it was not a difficult task.

Only Mother seemed unusually quiet and thoughtful. She appeared weary, and she rested frequently after exertion.

Robert was "Bob" to all of us except Dad; he always called him Robert. He was living with the family again, feeling the need to contribute towards the financial responsibilities. Bob always added sparkle to everyday living, and we were so glad to have him live at home again. He held a responsible job as a foreman in a nearby industrial plant, and this enabled him to increase his savings. His dating took on a more serious tone as he was searching for a wife. Surprisingly enough, he did not have to go far. After a lengthy engagement, he married the girl next door. She was a school teacher and a minister's daughter.

Betty was not only a popular teenager, but a beautiful one, too. After she graduated from high school, she entered a nursing school in Philadelphia. During her training she fell in love with an artist. He had a large advertising firm in center city. Betty enjoyed the excitement of city life and could no more tolerate a quiet little town. She married her artist and continued to live in Philadelphia. They had a lovely child — a daughter.

Noah was now nicknamed Bill (this did not please Daddy—he said he heard of too many horses called Bill!). Tall, blond and handsome with a debonair manner, he attracted all the ladies. He was employed in a food market; in time he became the manager. After some lively little romantic escapades, he finally settled down with a local girl. She filled his heart and home with love, and bore him two fine sons. For a short time he resided at "our hotel" on Grant Street.

Myles had a permanent position with a well known shoe company in Delaware. Later, he moved back to Lancaster to manage a branch store. He fell in love with a young lady who lived below Lancaster. After they were married they went south for a short time, then returned and resided with us until a suitable apartment could be found. They had one girl—a great delight to her daddy's heart.

Our togetherness worked out well. Surely it was providential that we shared responsibilities and enjoyed one another so much. Those years of congenial communication and friendly caring for one another are fragrant memories never to be forgotten.

Surely God deigned this togetherness, preparing us for future days when we would need and comfort one another, for a dark cloud overshadowed our home.

Chapter 20

All Is Not Well!

In the year of 1933, Mother's usual robust health showed a marked decline. It started with a severe cold and troublesome cough. The previous fall she had been examined for a lump in her breast. After a biopsy, the doctor pronounced it cancer; her breast had a malignant tumor. He also advised surgery, a mastotomy.

Unknown to her children, she had discovered the lump when still living in Florida. Fearing cancer and noticing no change, she ignored it.

Now Daddy was alarmed and urged her to consider an operation. Mother hesitated, knowing the enormous financial strain it would make on the family income. She also had a spiritual knowledge that to take such a step may cause untold suffering in the family. At last she consented. They removed the breast and surrounding tissues. Surgery was not the answer. The disease had metastasized and caused malfunctions of most of the organs. Radium treatments followed, but it was too late. The malignancy webbed the lungs, and destroyed the normal functioning of the vital organs.

Pain, labored breathing and severe nausea were her daily lot. Her days of suffering were beautiful examples of patience and acquiescence. She never cried out against her circumstances. She had accepted God's will. Day by day she would encourage us to be cheerful, to count our blessings and be thankful.

There it was again, I thought; "Blessings, blessings, where were they? How could one be thankful for the pain and declining health that was hers?"

Caring for her was a privilege. Kathryn and I took turns bathing and dressing her incision. At first, after her return from the hospital she spent much of the day sitting on her favorite rocking chair near a window in our living room.

This rocker emitted a rhythmic little tune which seemed to say to her "all is well, all is well." The sound irritated me: "All is not well!" I thought.

Once, having spent several hours up in my little art studio, I came downstairs to drink some cold buttermilk and relax a bit. Hearing the familiar little tune from her chair, I turned and entered the living room. Mother's face was flushed, her eyes were too bright; her temperature was up again, that was obvious. She welcomed me with a smile and inquired, "Did you finish the painting?" Her interest and enthusiasm was a constant source of encouragement. Often she asked me to paint bluebirds. How she loved bluebirds! I painted them for her on pillow cases, china, glasses and what-have-you. My dad was a competent artist and understood art. Mother simply enjoyed it, accepting it as it was.

The rocker "tune" continued to annoy me. I felt discouraged and depressed. My voice betrayed my feelings as I grumped, "no-o-o-o, not yet. It takes so long to catch depth in flowers."

Her eyes beckoned me to stay and visit with her. I found a comfortable chair and waited for her to speak again.

"Mae, will you do me a big favor? Remember my new dress, the navy one we made with ivory lace around the neck?"

"Yes, I remember. Why do you ask, Mother? Are you planning to go to church? I think it will be some time before you wear it." "Not yet," her voice came softly, "but I will be wearing it one more time. I would like to remove the old lace and have some new white lace put on. Will you find it in the lower part of my sewing box?"

Mother was sending out a hidden message but it by-passed me.

"All right, Mother," I whined reluctantly, "if you must have it done, but I don't see why we can't do it some other time." It only took a few moments to find the new dress and the sewing basket. Mother carefully took the razor blade which she used for ripping and neatly removed the lace. Handing the dress to me, she selected some new lace along with some thread and a needle. I fastened the lace to the edge of the collar, careful to avoid wrinkling the garment.

74

Between stitches I would glance at her as she slowly rocked. Her eyes were closed and her head was resting against the back of the rocker. Frustrated because of her illness, fear gripped my heart. What if she would die? Unable to face this fear and aware that I had no inner security, I felt guilty and constantly angry. I had little faith in prayer and wondered why God had it in for me? There was so much I wanted to share with her, but I could not. She was such a wonderful, sweet, and good mother. How could she ever understand the tumult of evil that seemed so much a part of me? I loved her so deeply and she surely must have known even if I rarely told her so.

I remember one time when she was on her rocker she asked me to come and sit on her lap.

"Mother, I'm seventeen now, no baby!" I exclaimed.

"Come sit here and you'll feel better. It's so long since I held you," she coaxed.

Drawn by her warm love I self-consciously sat on her lap in a sideways position. Quickly she drew me close to her warm breast, her loving arms around me. We were silent as she gently rocked to and fro. Oh, I loved the warmth of her full bosom, the mild fragrance of perfume that she wore, and her soft cheek pressed on my forehead.

Perhaps a dozen moments slipped by, then she whispered in my ear, "Can't you tell me what bothers you?"

I desperately wanted to. Wincing with inward pain and longing, I remained silent to her offer to help. I began gradually to move away from her loving embrace. Her eyes were glistening with tears, but she said nothing.

Snipping the threads from the finished garment, I handed the dress to her. Opening her eyes she smiled and said, "Thank you, Mae, that was neatly done." But my emotions were cross-stitched and knotted.

After days and nights of pain, her body became weaker until she was unable to sit out on her chair. Her breath became so labored that she could be heard a distance away from her room. We massaged her limbs, rearranged her pillows, and served all kinds of food to excite her appetite, but all was to no avail. The long, stitched scar was almost completely healed except for an opening under the arm which stubbornly refused to close.

One morning, while Kathryn and I were bathing Mother, we noticed this wound was closing. I thought, "This surely is a sign that she is getting better." On the contrary, this wound indicated the rejection of the body to battle and rebuild its own cells.

The last week in February was surprisingly mild. The sunbeams brightened the dark patches on the quilt as we gently tucked it about her shoulders. After her bath and a change of linens, she seemed brighter and more cheerful. Kathryn and I kept our conversation in a trivial vain, hoping to control the mounting anxieties we felt within us.

After checking the flowers and adding fresh water, I placed a lovely bouquet of carnations, daisies and pussy willows on Mother's night table. Our neighbors and friends kept her room bright with many beautiful arrangements—all tokens of love and concern.

I noticed her eyes rest on the flowers for a time, then she made this comment: "The flowers are bursting forth from the earth, where I shall return for a season . . . and again come forth in newness of life." This comment was like a knife to my soul.

Impulsively I reproved her with, "Why must you always think of death?" On the surface of my mind I rejected thoughts of death. No, she could not be taken from us! God, why must she suffer so?

We watched Daddy age before our eyes. He knew, he understood. But I refused to accept the inevitable. I reasoned, "It must be the enormous debt that worries him so."

Kathryn was carrying her second child, which promised to arrive in March. Her countenance was weary and downcast. Her eyes conveyed grief. She was torn between great joy for the new gift of life and impending gloom of sorrow and loss which would be ours in the days to come.

Chapter 21

God Has Other Plans

One morning Mother requested the anointing service which we Brethren practiced, found in James 5:13-16. Kathryn and I sat quietly at the foot of the steps so we could hear all that was being said. The ministers asked the usual questions before they performed this service. Brother Cassel and Brother Hershey were sympathetic and concerned as they spoke to our parents. First they inquired about faith. Was their faith great enough to believe God yet was able to perform a miracle and heal Mother? Addressing Mother, Brother Hershey said, "Minnie, do you desire to live?"

My cheeks flushed with anger. "How could they doubt her desire to live?"

She spoke softly between each labored breath. "Oh, yes, if it's His will, I would like to stay here with my beloved family . . . " Now, more faintly she added . . . "but He has other plans for me . . . " We could hear Daddy's grief even on the steps.

Then followed, "Is there any known sin you wish to confess at this time? Is everything right between you and your fellowmen?" Brother Hershey's voice trembled as he spoke.

My heart beat wildly in my troubled breast, torn thoughts ripped at my mind. "Why do they continue to question the integrity of my mother's life? Was she not a living example of Christian teaching?" I slipped up a step to better hear her reply, above the sound of my hammering heart, and Kathryn's stifled sobs.

It seemed so long until we heard in stronger tones, "No, there is no unconfessed sin, all is well with my soul . . . but I do need patience to endure, and grace for these days . . . "

The minister dabbed oil on her brow and both ministers proceeded to lay hands on her head. Brother Cassel solemnly invoked the Lord to touch and restore our dear Mother according to His mighty power and will. He added compassionate petitions for Daddy and the family as well. I did not wait to hear Brother Hershey's concluding prayer. Never had I heard my dad weep so greatly. Kathryn, so grief-stricken, was unaware that I slipped past her and made my way numbly out into the back yard. It was dusk, and the gentle shadows seemed to enfold me. Alone and desolate, my anger was spent. I stood motionless before my Great God . . . the same God who was going to put "blessings on my head!"

Several days passed and Mother seemed brighter. One afternoon I hurried up to Mother to show her the material I had bought and the pattern which seemed to go well with it. The fabric was a green flowered voile and a bit gayer in design than I ventured to wear previously. Eager to have her approval, I said, "Look, Mother, what I found. Isn't it a refreshing color? Here is the new pattern — it's really different from what I've worn before!"

She smiled as I handed her the fabric, and ran her fingers between the folds, feeling its texture and durability. Finally she remarked, "It is pretty material, but is it not a bit transparent and gay for you?" Her next statement was so profound . . . it still rings in my ears. "Early in life," she went on, "I became a Christian and had to learn to choose to serve either God or mammon."

I caught her concealed admonition and knew she was reminding me that I, too, would have this choice. I would have to decide, "Am I pleasing God, or following my own desires and thus pleasing the devil?" Later I followed my own dictates, but the green dress lost all its glamor.

March came in with its bleak, cold days, strong winds and sneaky little snow storms. The doctor's visits became more frequent. Mother's temperature remained high; coughing wracked her body. Intense pain took its toll. Emaciated and frail, her countenance still conveyed a serene expression of hope. She patiently endured the trial of faith that she might receive her crown with joy (II Timothy 4:8).

Repeatedly she spoke of God's will for her life and ours. I recall one morning as we were ministering to her needs she called our attention to her legs. "Feel how cold they are." A chill passed over me as I ran my hands over her cold skin.

Kathryn threw an agonized glance at me, and we frantically rubbed her limbs. We applied heat applications, but our efforts were useless.

Death stealthily was claiming this precious form. Even with this obvious fact my mind cried, "No-no, no, Mother, you can't leave us now!"

One day when the sun was breaking through the clouds with a promise of fairer weather, Mother noticed and gestured for me to come closer. Bending over her wasted form, I tenderly laid my hand on her brow and silently cried, "Oh, Mother, there is so much I need to tell you, but I cannot now!" She seemed to read my thoughts as her deep blue eyes rested on my face.

"Someday, Mae, someday . . . " she whispered. Then she motioned towards the window. Not understanding, I walked over to the nearest window, and waited. Her lips were moving and I knew she wanted me to raise the window. I hestitated because it was still cool outside. Again, she indicated her desire. Only then did I notice her luminous face and hear her whisper, "Let them in, please let them in!"

What had my mother seen? Were there angels descending from Glory that my earthbound eyes could not behold?

On one of the doctor's last visits Mother refused the pain-killing injections. When the doctor inquired why she refused to have this medication which would induce sleep and reduce her pain, she replied, "You see, I want to have a clear mind when my Lord comes for me." It was obvious the doctor was impressed and admired Mother's courage.

He patted her shoulder and said, "I understand. It won't be long anymore."

That evening Daddy informed us that Mother's last wish was to talk to each of us personally and as a family. We solemnly gathered around her bed. Restraining our grief, we took our places by her side and waited for her to speak. In turn she affectionately held our hands, with her eyes fixed earnestly on our faces. She tenderly whispered her personal messages to each of us. Her deepest longings were that we would live Godly lives, thereby assuring her heart we would be reunited in Heaven. Around her bedside we all received a message from

God more impressive than a sermon.

The emotional strain was too much for me. When it was my turn to stand by her bed my vision blurred and the room lost all proportion as I sank into unconsciousness.

When I came to, Kathryn was bending over me with a glass of warm milk and a pill. Slipping into a deep sleep I was oblivious to both the painful gasps coming from Mother's parched lips and the words of love and comfort Daddy uttered during that night.

When morning came Mother was barely cognizant of her surroundings. Her cheeks were ashen, her bright blue eyes were gazing into Eternity. Her visions were hidden to our earthbound sight. She was being "transported." With a radiant smile, she gazed upward and murmured, "He . . . He is coming . . . can't you see Him?" We strained to understand her words, which came slowly and faintly after a long pause . . . "in all His Glory with His angels . . . coming . . . to . . . take . . . me . . . Home." Death made its own sound as it moved into her wasted form.

A sob escaped Daddy as he slowly turned away from the bed. He said in a hushed voice, "She is Home with the Lord now."

Within I wailed, "God, God, God, Why? . . . Why? . . . Where is your compassion and mercy?" Insensitive to Daddy's need, I wrapped my soul in a blanket of bitterness and anger. How long I laid across my bed motionless I am unable to say.

Voices broke into my benumbed mind. A persistent knock on the door compelled me to get up and unlock it. Mrs. Knittle and Kathryn were waiting to come in. In a strangling wave of grief I said, "I know she's gone forever!" Mrs. Knittle was a pastor's wife and frequently had shown real concern for me. But this time I rejected sympathy. I did not want anyone now. Selfishly I neglected poor Kitty, who moved about so laboriously. The house had to be tidied, food prepared and notices sent to relatives and friends. I moved like a zombie through those dark and seemingly hopeless days. Tears were not mine to shed.

Out came the navy dress with its fresh lace collar to once more adorn the shell which had contained a warm, loving personality.

Daddy, buoyed by God's Spirit, found comfort in his hope. He calmly and quietly moved through this period, never questioning God's will. Only once I heard him wistfully say to my brother, "If only I could have gone with her."

My eyes were fixed on the casket as it was gently eased into the earth. "No, no, no!" The silent screams of my soul were so deafening. I heard none of the condolences that were sounded from the hearts of relatives and friends. I stiffly plucked a long-stemmed rose from a large wreath on the casket. Ah, the pain of its thorns were welcome compared to the ache of my heart. Engulfed in bitterness and disconsolate, I wondered how the family could converse so easily.

After we returned from the funeral services, my family endeavored to restore our home to its normal routine. Each one of us reacted sensitively to this great loss. She had a tremendous influence on our lives. The vacancy was keenly felt.

The Bible was a comfort and consolation to Daddy. Openly he wept as he claimed its unfailing promises.

Easter came early in April, adorned in the glory of New Life. Daddy knew her secrets; by faith he walked her blood-trailed path, he witnessed her strength and assurance in a Risen Lord. But my soul wore the black shroud of death and I knew not where to turn.

Chapter 22

A Soul Divided

Life in my late teens became a grim battle for me. It was not long before my physical condition prevented me from attending classes at school. A friend and former school teacher came in and tutored me three days a week. She was a wonderful person and challenged me in countless ways. I learned a great deal through her inspiration and encouragement.

When she was no longer able to continue her tutoring, I turned to books. I became an avid reader of science and literature, especially fiction. Reading provided an escape for me. I would identify completely with the characters and pretend I was in their world. Within my own life raged a constant battle of fears, mounting anxieties, resentment and anger. I was unable to participate in normal school activities, or release tensions through hard physical exercises. Feelings and emotions piled up, leaving me greatly depressed.

Deep down in my heart I questioned, "Why must it be my lot to have all these problems? Where were all these 'blessings' that dear Elder Moore prayed to come down on my head?"

For me, life was only an experience one had to endure. Secretly I would resort to my dream world, and there try to find satisfaction and comfort for my soul. Kathryn and Betty would often share their romantic experiences with me. I would simply borrow their experiences and relive them in my own colorful way. I was starved for fellowship with my own peers. Deprived and lonely, I turned to fantasies—fantasies within myself. Self became the person I both hated and worshipped.

After a while, I was unable to cope with this demanding spirit of mine. I was always grieving over my behavior. How often I heard others say, "Why do you look so sad?" Guilt stalked my heels. Anguish and desolation found expression through my pen and paint brush. Sheer darkness pervaded the halls of my mind and spirit.

It frightened me to recognize several personalities within. How could one be so divided? Quickly I learned to "don" the "outside Mae." This personality was the most rewarding. She was clever and could deceive everyone — almost, that is — except God. He was not deceived. Frequently, He would expose this reprobate to me.

I was aware of a tremendous need of stability and inner strength and control. No amount of self effort and discipline attained these virtures. I was still unable to tap the sources of strength which I so desperately needed, which I recognized and coveted in other lives.

There were periods when I found a measure of relief by expressing myself through the avenues of art and writing. Conflicts, hostility, rebellion and confusion were all uniquely expressed in my art work. My doctors claimed I was unusually gifted to catch such sensitivity and portray it so well. They gave me free treatments in exchange for my drawings.

Hospital visits were frequent. Tests of every description were tried. I was extremely nervous and high-strung. These experiences always left me worse and in a weakened condition. I adored my heart specialist. Once he remarked, "You have too much spirit for the temple!" He realized also that I had a deep spiritual problem and advised me to talk to my minister.

I followed his advice and came away disappointed. In fact, I worsened and withdrew even more from normal activities. Joining the family in the evening for games, or listening to radio programs, bored me. It was something we had always enjoyed doing together. I had little to share with others in conversation and cared less to hear what others said. To escape from painful reality was all I wanted. If only I could escape my self! Drugs became the answer.

In time I increased my doses. This was not hard to do because I cleverly arranged for different members of the family to take the same prescription to different drug stores to be refilled several times a week.

Soon I had more than an ample supply, much more than the required dose. After a period of time, my psychosomatic symptoms were hardly noticeable. I was oblivious to the "inner agonies," and frequently moved in an euphoric behavior pattern.

The heart specialist decided that it would be beneficial if I would spend several months in a convalescent home near the seashore. I both welcomed and dreaded this move. I welcomed it because I desperately longed to get away, away from the familiar things and people who found my declining health and frame of mind a burden and too complex to try to understand. My family was not lacking in sympathy or concern. Very likely my self-centeredness was so great that I could not readily sense reactions from others. So it was arranged that I go to a convalescent home in New Jersey.

Chapter 23

The Silver Feather

Atlantic City had a large convalescent home for women, one block from the shore line. After I arrived, it was easy to adapt myself to the schedule and routine of this pleasant rest home. The nurses were strict but friendly as they enforced the regulations. After a doctor's exam upon entering, we did not need his services unless we were ill and advised by the head nurse to call him. Miss Night was concerned for my welfare, and became more than a "head nurse" to me. She was a friend, and I grew to love her.

She would call a practical nurse and order a wheelchair. I was not permitted to take long walks alone. So up and down the boardwalk we would go, pausing at every window display, moving in and out of the various shops, fascinated by the unique and interesting curios, and art work. The riff-raff of society mingled with the elite.

Sometimes my practical nurse, whom I called Aunt Laura, would venture out on the sandy beach with me. The breathless wonder of the ocean enthralled me. Its mighty power was beyond human control. Its depth was unfathomed and vast areas unexplored. I remembered reading in Job (38:11) that God commands the waves "not one inch further . . . thou proud waves be stayed."

On warm days we would park the wheelchair under the boardwalk, remove our shoes and stockings and allow the cool green ebb to lick at our toes. Ooh, it was delightful! The salty air was like an atomizer spraying my face and pleasantly flavoring my lips. These daily excursions proved to meet more than one need of mine. Aunt Laura became a close friend. She sensed my deeper problems; as a mother she knew how to comfort me.

When I realized the three weeks were coming to an end, I did not want to return home. I had made a number of friends, including some of the other nurses. The house doctor suggested I remain for a month or two longer. It was obvious that I was improving. My expenses for the allotted time were paid by the state, (the home rarely kept any patient longer than three weeks on state rates). Auntie Laura began to negotiate for me. She felt she could persuade the staff to plead my cause. She was a deeply religious woman and had first-hand knowledge to God's answers to prayers. As she called on God, the men on the home board considered my case and finally concluded that I would be their "exception to the rule," and I was permitted to stay the extended time.

Exposed to Auntie's spiritual teachings and her abundance of love and concern, something within me began to thaw. The Word, which she constantly applied to each situation, penetrated my dull senses. I stubbornly resisted the spiritual stirrings within, but outwardly I was politely attentive.

God was at work. Does His Word not say, "He is the discerner of the thoughts and intents of the heart" (Hebrews 4:12)? Was it God's "blessings on my head" when He directed my path to cross Aunt Laura's . . . ? "Line upon line, here a little, there a little . . . ."

Sometimes she became tedious, sometimes repetitious, until I indicated I was bored and weary. No matter how cleverly I manipulated the conversation, she invariably found some reason to inject God into the subject.

Auntie was an English lady by birth. Her delightful accent was both pleasing and amusing. As she often said, "My 'art and my 'ome are open to everybody." She used her practical nurse's training in her retirement years to win others to her Saviour. But my heart was not receptive or willing to hear His call.

In spite of every environmental improvement, all I could show for my stay at the rest home was a wee gain in weight—about three pounds. The thought of returning home discouraged me greatly.

The last week of my stay I sank into a deep depression. I grew more silent and withdrawn. I avoided Aunt Laura on the sun porch and refused our usual walks. My food became distasteful and I barely touched it. Nights were nightmarish.

My only thoughts were to escape, escape from the familiar scenes, home relatives and the unbearable restlessness which tormented me so.

Tuesday evening of the last week at the home I was so desperate I feared for my mind. After sipping a half glass of milk at the table, I excused myself and hurried to my room. Sleep, that was the answer. I would sleep! I would escape the clawing fears and anxieties which tormented me so. I collapsed on my bed, helplessly.

My sudden disappearance from the dinner table was reported to Miss Night. She wasted no time to seek the reason for my behavior. Before I said "come in" to her persistent tap on the door, I frantically searched for a truthful answer, not wishing to divulge my mental anguish and turmoil.

Calm and dignified, she entered my room. Her eyes were fixed on my face. "Mae, is something troubling you?" Always professional, yet capable of great kindness.

I left the room and down the long hall unnoticed and unconcerned about rules and regulations. It was the social hour period, and everyone who was able met downstairs for snacks and entertainment. I slipped quietly out of the back entrance marked, "Private, For Nurses Only."

A path led to the beach, ran under the boardwalk and directly to the shore. The tide was in. Waves lapped greedily at the rim of the shore. Sand birds were surfing the tide's foamy green residue, as it glaced the sandy shore. Spellbound, I watched these little creatures as they dipped into the slimy drainage for succulent morsels of food. Each wave sucked great draughts of sand, then swallowed noisily as it receded back into the ocean depths again.

I waded slowly into the cool water. As the tide ebbed away, I could feel the sand drain from my shoes and stockings. Clammy strings of seaweed webbed around my ankles. I watched darkness blur the horizon, majestic waves, like

"Not exactly," I swallowed hard, "it's just that I'm very tired, and I thought I'd go to bed."

Not daring to look at her, I closed my eyes. Tears stung my lids as I waited for her to leave. She was skeptical; I could feel it.

After a time she said, "I'll let you rest, but not before you take your pill."

She brought hot milk, and the pill was obediently swallowed. I heard her gently close the door. Scalding tears overflowed and wriggled their way across my face, leaving moist blobs on my pillow. How long I sobbed in my pillow I do not know. Shades of night were descending . . . and I was alone, dreadfully alone.

The rhythmical pound of the waves sounded loud and clear through the windows of my mind. Weary and exhausted, I pulled myself up and moved off the bed. The walls of the room seemed too close. I must escape. My fluttering heart and spirit wanted to soar as the sea gull—away, away from it all. An uncontrollable desire possessed me, compelled me to "take flight." I would flee from my home, my relatives, yes, and my despised body which imprisoned my restless spirit. But where would I go?

white-tipped mountains, crashed and thundered towards me. Soon they collapsed and broke into mini waves and they, too, fiercely lashed the shore.

My wet skirt fastened its cold skin to my limbs, and the stinging sprays were bone chilling, but I disregarded all this discomfort. Were not those waves beckoning me? Beckoning . . . beckoning . . . me . . . the voices of the sea? Drawn by their hypnotic sounds, I inched my way towards them. The heavens were dark and only the yellowish lights from the boardwalk glistened faintly and impersonally.

As each receding wave sucked and pulled at my weary frame, I worked my shoes deeper into the ocean's floor, barely able to keep my balance. I became aware that I must make a quick decision. The heave of the waves was too powerful for me.

Was this the summons? Did they not offer release? Trembling now, and wavering like the seaweed tossed to and fro, I turned my face to heaven. Desperate breakers broke over my soul. "God, oh God," I cried, "is this all there is for me . . . darkness, endless emptiness?" "If You can help," I screamed above the din, "show me a sign." My words seemed to be swallowed up in the night and, by the thinnest moment, lost.

Then suddenly I heard a "soft swish" above the pandemonium! There, almost brushing my wet cheek, was the most beautiful white sea gull. It circled above me gracefully; then, dipping lower, it dropped a silvery feather right on my hand.

Somewhere, within or without, I knew not where, I heard these words: "Turn, my child, this is not My summons, and I will help you out of the darkness."

With supernatural strength I turned and moved towards the shore, conscious now of God's undertaking for me. He had won the battle, subdued the enemy of my soul. Then I was aware of the anxiety and concern I may have caused the nurses at the home. With haste I retraced my steps; I reached the rear door and was dismayed to find it locked. Soaked to the bone and shivering, I rang the bell.

When Miss Night discovered it was me, she wept. Putting her arms around me she led me upstairs, undressed me and tucked me in bed. Pulling a chair close to the bed, she quietly waited for me to talk. We talked until the wee hours. It was like a healing balm.

Auntie Laura did not pry the next day and I did not avoid her, but she knew and coached me in prayer.

A thoughtful young woman returned home with a deeper conviction that God heard and answered prayer, and with a pearly white feather to demonstrate His care.

Chapter 24

A Prisoner Tossed To and Fro

Daddy did not refute our suggestions that he should go to Florida over the winter months. His bronchial problems returned and he coughed day and night. Obviously his health was failing and he realized this, along with the fact that he was very lonely. So he agreed to go south.

Our large house was slowly being evacuated, its occupants moving to various places. Kathryn and her family found a home in a nearby village. Myles and his wife moved into a home down on Main Street. Sister Betty, now married also, had moved to a residential section outside of Philadelphia. Bob and Mary moved into a two-story house on Charlotte Street. I was to stay with them, at least for a time. Dad would make his home here over the summer. My sister-in-law arranged a nice room for me to occupy. In turn, I helped with the household chores whenever possible. My months spent here were unhappy ones. With frequent visits to the doctor, hospital admissions and prolonged bed rest periods, this was too much for me to cope with.

The doctor finally advised a change. I was to spend a month in a lovely convalescent home down near Coatesville. I willingly agreed to go. Perhaps here I would find what I was searching for. The home was rather a pretentious place. Its acres of well kept lawns rose and fell over gentle hills. Countless shade trees spread their graceful arms over the weak and the frail. Fuchsia, lavender and purple rhododendron spread their ballerina skirts in gay profusion over earth's luscious jade rug. We were serenaded each morning by the birds. Here nature herself poured out serenity and healing.

In this home the patients were a bit more sophisticated and aloof than in the Atlantic City one. One could become lonely even in these restful surroundings. Making friendly overtures was worth my efforts. There were times when my heart listened and I heard the silent cry of another heart. I heard this cry when I found my dear friend Harriet. She was not of the common run of humans. Her independent spirit and bubbling sense of humor were most refreshing. Perhaps it was our mutual health problems that first drew us together. Furthermore, we recognized deep spiritual needs in the other. As we opened our hearts and minds in sharing, our friendship was strengthened. Prayers, tears, joys and laughter sealed a lifelong friendship.

After I left the convalescent home, I visited with Kathryn for a short time. Again, there was a new problem. Bob and his family were leaving the Charlotte Street home. They decided to move on a farm located some distance from Manheim.

When I learned of their plans I was heartsick. This town was home to me. My church, although I rarely attended, was a source of security. The members were friends and were so kind to me. Many were cousins, first, second, and third. Also a number of aunts and uncles were included. Graybills, Hersheys, Gibbles and Longeneckers made up the greatest part of the White Oak Church. We were all interrelated and these dear folks were my only source of social contact. But I had to live with Bob because there was no other home available for me.

The large farm house that Bob's family occupied was originally a two-family dwelling. Since Kathryn had to move again, she eagerly accepted her older brother's invitation to come and occupy the other side of this farm house.

When Kathryn and her family joined us on the farm, my spirits lifted for a time. We spent much time together, and her loving heart accepted some of my burdens. But this was a very short period. Without any social contacts, I sank into my troublesome self again. Sometimes I felt like a prisoner. Unfortunately, I was so blinded with self pity I could not recognize I was a prisoner of myself! Kathryn's reminders that "God could do the impossible for me" rolled off my ears like drops on a duck's back. Nor had I the spiritual insight to accept what must have been "blessings on my head." Here on the farm I could find nothing to divert my thoughts.

I worsened, emotionally. Clouds of despair and fear hung

darkly over my head, and I became somewhat paranoid. Each day brought a greater struggle to maintain my equanimity. Extreme anxieties and bizarre feelings mounted until it was unbearable. I begged to see a psychiatrist. My family arranged an appointment for me. I was in such a frightful condition that the doctor recommended that I should enter a hospital where my emotional and physical problems could be carefully studied.

Chapter 25

God Woos the Wandering Heart

After three weeks of negotiating with the Philadelphia Institute, an appointment was made for me to enter. My church assumed a great part of the financial responsibility; otherwise I would have been unable to go. One paid dearly for such individual care and treatment.

Specialized men in all fields of medicine were consulted. Here graduate doctors came for training.

Bob and Myles drove me to the hospital and took care of my financial obligations and admission papers.

The lobby of this hospital was a most impressive place. Its interior denoted elegance — a true replica of a drawing room in an old mansion. All the suites and rooms were furnished to create a home-like atmosphere.

The food was delicious and included gourmet dishes. Fresh flowers were placed daily on each tray. In addition to all these personal touches, we had special nurses who appeared in street clothes; they were always available to assist us even for our smallest needs. My own nurse had the most congenial personality. She helped me to accept my strange surroundings and adjust more easily.

In the past I was plagued with nightmares and would walk in my sleep. This occurred one night after a day of countless tests and emotional strain. It was about one-thirty a.m., I was told, that I put on my bathrobe and walked down the hall to the elevator. Operating the elevator to the first floor, I promptly stepped out into the lobby and headed for the front entrance. The girl at the desk recognized me and alerted my nurse. The competent little nurse maneuvered the episode so smoothly that I could hardly believe it happened.

The occupational department offered all kinds of courses. We were encouraged to participate and become involved in these classes. I enthusiastically selected the art course. Imagine my chagrin when our instructor had chosen a naked male as our model for our first two lessons! This was too brazen for my delicate disposition. With burning cheeks, I hastily retreated from the class.

Back in my room I re-focused the scene in my mind. Shocked and confused, I wondered . . . "Is this realistic art . . . ? Was I unable to accept facts?" Exposure to nudity was sinful to me. It was related to the wretched battle within.

How could I detach my emotions from my body? I could not. Why was I trembling so?

Caught in the churning, conflicting tide . . . only one way out . . . no, I will not sink into that cesspool . . . no! Quickly I reached for the yellow capsules on the dresser. The warm water from the bathroom aided the capsule's descent, and I slipped into oblivion.

About ten o'clock p.m. I awakened . . . calm . . . and in my night clothes. Evidently the nurse had undressed me and tucked me back in bed. On the night table was a glass of milk and some fresh fruit.

A dear young girl occupied the room next door to me. She was so lonely. Frequently I would stop by and chat with her. She was the finished product of affluence. Her parents were famous and quite wealthy. They offered her everything her little heart could desire . . . except their love. She was raised by a governess.

Sue had a beautiful large photo of a collie setting on her dresser. It was her dog, and she loved it dearly. But two months previously the dog had become ill and died. The girl never left the dog's side during its three weeks of illness. After her pet's death, her world fell apart.

Her relationship with her mother was very strained. Part of the treatment at the institute was to help her accept her mother. The mother was a beautiful lady with large, sad eyes. Daily she visited with Sue, always bringing an expensive present, hopeful that in this way she could win her daughter's love and respect. With all these overtures of love, Sue remained alienated and indifferent.

At times her parents would take her out for an evening of entertainment. She would return in the same listless mood and begged not to go out with them again.

Every conceivable space in her room was filled with a facsimile of a dog. They were all shapes and sizes. Some were made of the most expensive materials and were a rare lot and most fragile.

One afternoon, after her usual visit with her mother, I waited in my room for her to join me. We had planned to have our dinner on the sun porch. Suddenly, it sounded like bedlam had broken loose next door. Her fine voice, high and shrill, was polluting the air with vulgar language. Smashing and banging punctuated her words . . . .

I was so shocked I couldn't move. Then I realized the storm was over and only muffled sobs could be heard. Debating whether to call a nurse, or try to comfort her myself, I decided on the latter. Softly I tapped on her door. I did not know what I would find, but I felt I could help her in some way. Receiving no answer, I gently turned the knob and entered the room. Crouched in the debris of her broken dogs, she wept inconsolably.

"Sue," I whispered, "It's Mae; I came to help you."

Her sobs subsided as I gently helped her into bed. Moments passed, then she turned her sad face towards me. I caught the silent scream from her heart; there was an empathy within me for this dear girl. My heart reached out to help . . .

"Sue, you are an avid reader, but have you ever read the Bible?"

Apathetically she shook her head. "No, why do you ask?"

I wanted so badly to help her; was not the Bible the Book to turn to in time of trouble? So I continued persuasively.

"I've read it, and it has words in there that really comfort and help. Some even say it has an answer to everyone's question. After all, it's about God, and He knows everything."

I sincerely believed this, although I had never deeply searched within its covers for answers to my own problems. My words were like darts that scored. Reason brightened her dull eyes as they rested on my face.

I removed the small Gideon Bible which was placed on a table in each room and paged through its tissued leaves. My eye rested on Psalm 41 and I began to read the verses aloud.

She quietly listened as I continued to the end. After a moment, I added, "I've read different chapters, and they tell us that other people have problems just like ours. So we are not the only people who hurt inside."

I was surprised and a bit embarrassed to hear myself say, "Sue, are you a Christian?"

She took the book from my hand and without looking at me she replied, "What is a Christian? I'm of German-Italian descent, if that's what you mean." And, as an added thought to prove her point, "Mother said I was baptized as a baby in the Catholic Church."

"No," I stammered, "I don't mean exactly that. The Bible teaches us God must enter the heart to be a true Christian."

"I know very little about religion. But how does God come into the heart?"

Now I was in deep water! How could I explain something that I did not fully understand myself? For some strange reason, John 3:16 popped into my mind. Childhood memory verses I had learned! John 3:16 was one verse Bible school teachers used each year — no matter how many times we learned it. So I had gleaned the meaning "by rote" of this verse.

I quoted the verse slowly and clearly. "For God so loved the world that He gave His only begotten Son, that whosoever believeth on Him shall not perish, but have everlasting life."

I did not realize that God used me to witness for Him, thus presenting Christ to this dear one for the first time.

As we continued to discuss the meaning of these words, she got off the bed and began to pick up the broken pieces. We soon had collected the larger pieces and put them in the waste basket.

It was late, and the last bell rang for dinner. Before I turned to go I promised to call and have a light lunch sent up to her room. I would also stop at the desk and ask for a cleaning lady to check Sue's room. More importantly, I promised to pray for Sue. In a few weeks I would be leaving, but who would help Sue find a way out of her misery? Then I recalled . . .

"If ye seek me ye shall find me," Jeremiah 29:13. Someday she would find Him. Oh, yes, I mentally corrected the verse.

"If ye seek me *with all your heart,* ye shall find me." "All of your heart" was not for me yet . . . , maybe someday . . . How patiently God woos the wandering heart.

After a six-week period of study and treatment, I showed some improvement. Financially I was unable to remain the allotted period of time. There was one aspect in my case history that perplexed my doctors. In a letter to my dad, they recommended a program of continual medical treatment, and they suggested the possibility there was a deeply rooted spiritual conflict. Perhaps counseling with a minister would be helpful.

At various times my doctors had commented about the unusual insight and ability I had to understand my emotional problems. This, they claimed, was my saving grace.

Once again I returned home utterly frustrated and completely convinced of the futility of it all! So I had a spiritual problem, and who was going to solve it?

I saw myself in a quagmire; the more I struggled to be free, the deeper I sank! God seemed so far away. For years I read my Bible, but only verses like these became meaningful to me: "Why hast thou cast me off?" I cried. Psalm 74:1, "Can You restore what has been ruined? Hast my soul's enemy destroyed the inner sanctuary where God can speak to man? Is there no acceptance of my offering?"

Sometimes I would walk out into our orchard after all my housework was done. It was a secluded place for me. Up on the highest limb of a tree I dared to climb. Here I found a measure of relief. How I enjoyed the sense of being somewhere between heaven and earth. I always felt inspired to paint or write poetry. Yes, even to pray. The trees were like friends. They, too, felt the need to reach up and search for God. Were not their great arms stretching upward for more strength and power?

Like them, I too stretched my arms up to the cerulean sky and cried, "Are you there, God, can you hear my voice?"

Sometimes it was like strong wine in my veins, a rapturous experience mingled with piety. Did God really say what I imagined I heard? Even in my valleys of despair, it was the same message. "'My child, am I not enough . . . have I not kept your little bark from shipwreck?"

"Yes," I thought, "It is remarkable that I am still capable of reasoning." This was like a glimmer of hope penetrating my darkness.

My heart responded with this plea.

When with Nature my soul seeks solitude,
While the wind breathes through my hair,
Lifting my arms up to the infinite blue,
I whisper a pleading prayer,
Dear God, of immortal powers, have You—
A grain to spare of courage, hope, or faith,
So that I may face life anew?

Chapter 26

Opportunities to Witness

It was over a year since Harriet and I had met. But we kept in touch with one another. She lived in the city about eight miles from our home. When she learned of my loneliness and unhappiness, she and her mother decided I should come and live with them for a while.

Her mother had a heart of gold. She not only took me into her home, but into her heart as well and treated me like a daughter. One of the happiest surprises of my life was when she bought me the most beautiful dressing gown I had ever seen. Its delicate blue background had dainty pink roses scattered all over it. A sweetheart neckline and tiny puffed sleeves made it ultra feminine. The soft flowing full skirt rustled gently with every move as it swished over my blue satin slippers. Wee roses exactly like those in the gown were painted on the toes. I tied my long hair back with a blue ribbon, and I felt like a princess!

On one occasion that I took it with me to the hospital, it brightened my whole two-weeks stay. Perhaps I stood out a bit more than others in that twelve-bed ward. On the third day there, I was moved out on the solarium. There it was like having a private room. Young, handsome interns would come out for a smoke to escape the pressures for a few minutes. Sometimes one or two nurses found time to join us. (This particular time I was in for dental surgery.)

We would have the nicest times laughing and talking about many things. Some of those interns caused me to have palpitations of a different sort!

One night the ward was unusually busy, and I was sitting on a rocker wishing someone would drop by. Who should come through the door but my favorite doctor. In a somewhat harassed voice, he asked, "Would you like to do me a favor?"

Welcoming a chance to do something for him, I readily

said, "Yes, I'd be glad to."

"Are you feeling up to it?" He hastily added.

"Sure, I need a bit of exercise," then I followed him through the ward. In bed number nine I assisted him in relieving a teenager of a cast that was troubling her. In bed number three a patient needed a clean dressing on her appendix incision.

I learned to know the nurses fairly well, so frequently I was permitted to enter the supply room to fetch sterile needles and other supplies.

This one night was unusually exciting. The ambulance siren screamed in a terrifying manner as it careened into the emergency driveway. White-coated aides hopped around like puppets as they removed the patient from the ambulance and rushed her into the clinic. From the fourth floor my view was lost as the whole scene was swallowed up inside the closed doors.

Out in the ward a bed was being prepared. Intravenous feeding paraphernalia was set up, and other emergency preparations were going on. Curtains were drawn around the bed as a patient was rolled in. Nurses were hurrying back and forth in the most urgent manner. Each one donned a gown, gloves and mask before they entered the enclosed curtains. My curiosity was increasing as I waited for a friendly nurse to come by and share a bit of information.

Seated at the open doorway I could hear this new patient's whispered mumblings. In a louder tone, I heard, "Hail, Mary, Mother of Jesus, save me now." It was sad to hear her continuous call for help, and I was moved to tears as I listened to her pitiful cries. "Pray for me—save me, save me."

I walked out of the ward and headed for the nurses' station. The large clock on the wall pointed to 1:00 a.m. This meant the head nurse would be down at the other end of the hall. As I walked into the nurses' station, only one nurse was there—a tiny blond "probe" with short curly hair. She was checking the charts. I started to speak when she interjected, "Wouldn't you know we'd get a patient who requires isolation, and we have no room to put her in. Besides, I'm the only one on the floor until three o'clock, and I have more than twenty others to look after."

After these remarks, I was all the more concerned, and I vowed I'd help this patient some way. I knew I was breaking the rules when I dared to ask to talk to the patient.

The nurse hesitated, then quickly glancing at her watch she moved to the supply closet and grabbed a gown, mask and gloves. Passing them to me, she whispered, "Don't get too close and don't stay long."

Donning the gown, gloves and mask, I walked into the ward and carefully slipped inside the curtains of bed number six. The "Hail Marys" came more slowly now. The patient must have been in her late twenties. Her waxy, white hands across her breast were moving restlessly as they fingered a rosary. Her large, dark eyes were glassy as they stared at the wall. A gray pallor settled over her face, and I shivered a bit as I realized there were more than two within that enclosed space. Death was there ready to claim its victim.

Gently I laid my hand on her fevered brow. She made the slightest movement with her head. Somewhere past the shadows of great pain and weakness she sensed my loving concern. Those eyes, so sunken, dark with fear, turned imploringly towards me.

In the faintest whisper she pleaded, "Please, please, help me, I'm lost. I have sinned much. There is no one to pay my way out of purgatory, no one to pray for me." A long sigh escaped her lips. She waited helplessly, her dark eyes begging yet fearful.

Reaching for the Bible which was placed in the top drawer, I found the 23rd Psalm. As I tried to comfort this dying woman, I unconsciously identified with her. Under my exquisite little blue gown beat a desperately longing heart that was also seeking peace and assurance. I had learned the 23rd Psalm by memory as a child. Still I felt the need to read it to her.

Softly and tenderly I began to read. "The Lord is my Shepherd I shall not want . . . " Then she murmured something like: "Am I really His sheep? How could He love me when I have sinned so? I . . . I ran away . . . they are hunting for me . . . " With a huge sigh she continued, "Please don't tell them I'm here . . . please." Fear tightened her lips and darkened her beautiful eyes.

"No . . . no," I assured her. "I shall never report you. No one will report you again." She need never know that an officer of the law had already received a report concerning her.

Once again I began to read the 23rd Psalm, ". . . I shall not want . . . He leadeth me in paths of righteousness . . . "

Then again she spoke. "I once was a devout nun . . . innocent to the ways of men . . . Oh, can God forgive me . . . twice I bore a child . . . two little graves left behind . . . the . . . " I heard mumbled words again. I waited patiently as she struggled for breath.

Then I prayed aloud, "God, help this woman to find peace, to know You have forgiven her before she dies." The silence now was broken by slow, deep, gurgling sounds. Placing my hands over hers as they held the crucifix, I whispered, "Do you believe Jesus died for your sins?"

I heard a faint "Yes."

". . . that only He can forgive your sins — no one else can do this for you?"

Again, I heard a weak but definite "Yes."

Her eyes were fixed on mine, and I saw a ray of hope and full accord with what I was saying.

Leaning closer to her, I continued softly, "If you really believe this, repeat these words after me." With the barest nod of her head I knew she understood. "Lord Jesus, I believe You died for my sins. Will You come into my heart as my Saviour? Will you forgive my many sins and wash me clean with your blood and save me?"

Between short breaths her faltering words repeated what I said . . . on to the end. As I watched the hostility, the fear and anguish fade, a gentle peace seemed to change her countenance. I knew then Christ had touched her and healed her as He tenderly accepted her confession. This scene was a never-to-be-forgotten one. The luminous glow about her face transformed the marks of sin into the face of a saint.

The curtains suddenly parted as two nurses came in to work with her. I quickly replaced the Bible and returned to my bed out in the solarium. How refreshing the night air was compared to the odor of rotting flesh!

I laid down with a weary sigh and pondered over all the "whys." Why did this dedicated young nun have to die in disgrace? Alone, hunted by the police and church officials, knowing only shame and sorrow; was there no one who cared?

Why was I able and willing to help her find the peace I was looking for? Wide-eyed, I stared into the starlit night, waiting for an answer.

The city hall tower chimed its fourth hour—morning would soon be here. Then I heard the squeak of wheels and rubber-soled shoes of nurses and doctors. Another light was on inside the curtains. I could see there was much activity. The curtain ballooned, then parted, as a stretcher with a still form was hurried out of the ward. No one needed to tell me what was going on. I knew the Lost Sheep was gathered into the Fold.

Chapter 27

New Adjustments

Harriet's home life differed considerably from mine. Being accepted in this fun-loving household, I soon began to unwind. I laughed freely and played games with interest. Here I participated in things that were forbidden at home. Harriet's brother taught me how to waltz and to enjoy classical music. We played cards in the evening. At meals sometimes we were served wee goblets of delicious wine. Her mother always encouraged me to imbibe, as it was good for my health. She was a nurse and it did not take much persuasion for I found it to be delicious! Because all these indulgences were done so modestly and this family manifested wholesome happiness, I had very little trouble with my conscience.

Dinner in the evening was rather formal and served on the whitest linen with initialed heirloom silver. Their grandma was a tiny little lady with a straight back and a quick step. She was a marvelous cook as well as a dominant figure in the home. She demanded the respect of every member of the family. Her words were few, but always worth listening to. The kitchen was her throne, and each of us respected her wishes. No one could wash dishes correctly, so she claimed the honors. Silverware always had to be dried two times, then neatly laid on a clean towel to thoroughly dry! In her middle eighties, she could still boast of never having a headache. We all loved her dearly.

With all the loving attention this beloved family shared with me, there was still a vacancy within. There were times when we had serious discussions concerning our spiritual needs, but their theories and ideas never coincided with mine. I could not accept the teaching that one could be a moderate worldling and still claim the righteousness of Christ. I did not understand why I felt so strongly about the few scriptures I knew, but for several years I had read my Bible through as a spiritual performance. It was something I could boast about. The verses became familiar, but the meaning was "Greek" to me!

During my stay with Harriet, I learned of a doctor who needed a receptionist. He lived only a short distance from this home. Harriet's mother encouraged me to apply for the position since it was only a part-time job. This worked out well, and I really enjoyed the responsibility.

The job was only available for eight months. At the end of this period I was very unhappy to find myself unemployed. Also Harriet's household had made some changes and I had to leave their home and find a place to live again.

On the corner of South Main Street in Manheim, Myles and his family occupied the smaller part of a double house. This dwelling was owned by an elderly couple, who were well established in the cabinet-making business and highly respected in our community.

These folks were always attired in simple clothes. "Plain folk" is what we called them. They were fine Christians and lived exemplary lives. Myles and his wife were employed, and this dear little grandmother would babysit for them.

When my brother learned that I longed to move back to Manheim, he and his wife agreed to my moving in with them. In return I would babysit, cook their meals and be as helpful as I could. What a delightful little niece I had. We spent many happy times together.

Myles felt his daughter should have a pet. So pets she had, like fluffy chicks, a waddling duck, a rabbit, a huge dog and a goat, no less! Sometimes my niece would invite these creatures into the house. Often we were hilariously entertained, then there were other times when we had catastrophies!

Most of the time that I lived with Myles I was employed as an artist for a Christian book store. I painted Bible verses and flower designs on glass, such as mottoes and mirrors. This work I would do after meals and in the evenings. My employer was a minister and a tremendous blessing to me. Both he and his wife became very dear friends of mine.

Here on Main Street our good neighbors shared our joys and woes with us. I learned to love this dear, elderly couple, and we were almost like a family. Our kitchen doors were only ten feet apart, and each door faced the other. On a warm summer day, when doors and windows were open, I heard these aged saints pray. This was not unusual.

Since the grandfather had been ill, we would hear him pray rather frequently. One time in particular I discerned more emotion in his tones than usual. I listened quietly to his supplication and praises and marveled over the length of his prayer, when suddenly his ecstatic words took on a strange, wailing sound. Words, they certainly were not! These sounds frightened me, and I was sure that he must be afflicted and in great pain, or suffering from a stroke!

With great concern, I hurried over to their kitchen; not finding anyone there I moved quickly through the other rooms to the front of the house. Then I saw them seated side by side. His head was tilted upward; with eyes closed and his arms upraised, he continued to wail and moan. His wife's face was wreathed in smiles, yet tears ran down her withered cheeks. Astonished and puzzled, I whispered, "Is he in pain?"

She sobbed a bit and motioned, "Sh-sh-h-h." Then, with a negative shake of her head she added horsely, "No-no-no, he chust has a 'glory spell' and is praising the Lord."

This was my first lesson in understanding what "getting happy" meant, from a religious point of view.

Chapter 28

Depression Returns

During the years I stayed in Myles' home I was keenly aware that I was one too many there. Since they only had two bedrooms and one unenclosed commode, none of us had the desired privacy we needed.

My little niece was old enough to have a bedroom of her own. But considering the whole situation, we got along fairly well.

My physical problems caused some concern, but my emotional behavior was utterly frustrating to them. Like in many families, tensions can become almost explosive. For me, a culmination of significant and insignificant incidents built up to a ridiculous degree. These self-accusations became vehicles of blame and defeat. I realized I should be out on my own. I wanted desperately to rent a small apartment or a room. This was almost impossible for the price I could pay. To lessen this feeling that I was imposing, I made more effort to help with the work and I discreetly cut down on my eating. With less nourishment, I naturally weakened physically. I lost the joy of meeting people, of responding to color and sound. My artistic talents seemed to fade.

Somewhere within me was a hunger, a panting for a divine touch, but I did not recognize it as such. Two natures seemed in conflict within, and I was confined, unable to escape their incompatibility.

Hopelessly imprisoned, I scarcely cared for anything but death. On rare bright days I would ponder this question. "Could God really help me if He wanted to? If He could heal my body, what about my soul's need? Does he not care that I am suffering so?" No one seemed to understand that my desire for inner healing was greater than a physical healing.

For all the discussions I had with the clergy, and there were a number, not one had enough spiritual insight to discern my deep spiritual needs. I sincerely searched within for a simple way to explain my tormented soul; I wanted clear answers for my mind and heart. More times than not I would hear words like these.

"Mae, you are a Christian, then why do you trouble yourself so? You take communion when you are able, you confess your sins, don't you? You believe in the doctrine which our church teaches and the required disciplines we are to obey. You pray. So what more can we say? Continue to trust God to help you, do good when you are able, love God and your fellow man, and let the rest up to Him."

In my mind a large neon sign glared back at me. What a facade I am! "Yes," I reasoned, "I believed the doctrines of the church. At least, I accepted them in my head. Jesus Christ was the Son of God and became Saviour for all those who accepted Him as such. His vicarious suffering and death could only become effective in the lives of those who believed this truth. Maybe it was effective for me thirteen years ago when I was baptized, but I could not witness to any changes or a sense of forgiveness. If God forgave me, why am I continuing to sin?"

With all this "rote" knowledge, I was pitifully lacking. For instance, I knew the Holy Spirit was a part of the Trinity. But that He would indwell a believer's heart was an unfamiliar reality to me. My eyes and ears were unenlightened, and I was unaware of this wonderful Personality who could change a life completely.

I would respectfully listen as my spiritual counselors tried to comfort me and explain reasons for my guilt and failures. These men of God meant well, but in the deep recesses of my soul things remained unchanged. I was a hopeless prisoner. My life was empty. No arm to lean on, no one to care, no fountain for cleansing . . . no healing there . . . echoes, echoes . . . echoes. Thus wept my soul in deep despair.

My sister Kitty was so concerned, but her hands were tied and she could do little for me. What she did do was the most important thing of our lives.

She had four lovely kiddies and one on the way, which kept her more than occupied. She was a devoted mother. Her visits were few, but her letters came faithfully. This one particular letter told of a dear friend with whom she had shared a prayer request concerning my health.

This friend had a fresh touch of God upon her life. A "spiritual heart transplant," she called it, and she was wonderfully transformed. She formerly had been a listless and indifferent wife and housekeeper. Now she manifested a zeal and a power that changed her whole lifestyle.

After receiving Kitty's prayer request, she felt led to write to me, being certain the Lord was directing. I received a lengthy epistle. Much of it contained scripture. She explained many verses and pointed out the ones I was to claim for healing. She included instructions on knowing if one is born again, on realizing the presence of the indwelling Holy Spirit.

No one had ever questioned me about this matter before. This approach was a bit upsetting to me. I was not willing or even interested in the Holy Spirit, nor was I ambitious enough to search the scriptures as she advised. This whole truth about an indwelling Holy Spirit more or less confused me. I didn't want to know more about Him.

I had been assured by my ministers that I had fulfilled all the disciplines and doctrines that my church required. Laying her letter aside, I dismissed this Holy Spirit stuff; it was not for me. I had heard of a few people who claimed they had the Holy Spirit. They behaved so strangely that others questioned their sanity! Furthermore, I figured it would not be long until I would be removed from all this inner turmoil—so why become involved?

Kitty's friend inferred that my time may be limited. Was this an indication that the doctor had already informed my family? This fact added fuel to my languishing will to live.

In the meantime Kitty had written to Betty and asked her to come and stay with me for several weeks. Since she was a nurse her time was limited, but she came for a short time. I appreciated the time she spent with me, but we did not enjoy a close relationship as sisters at that period of our lives.

A dear friend of mine was so concerned for me that she asked permission to call in a specialist who lived in Harrisburg. He was a reputable neurologist who had previously been consulted about my case. His required fee for an office call was far beyond my financial means. Dr. Abbit knew all this, but knowing this did not deter his willingness to help me.

My family was deeply grateful for his generosity. Furthermore, they were reassured that I was receiving the very best care. His appointment with me was on Monday morning at ten. Saturday and Sunday passed meaninglessly. Monday came with some apprehension. I took a rather dim view of Dr. Abbit's visit.

Arriving promptly at ten, he entered our living room bearing that distinguished air of gentle refinement. Tall, erect and immaculate in British tweeds, he moved with ease across the room. Moving a straight chair, he placed it beside my sofa. His manner was so flavored with fatherly concern, it was difficult to realize he was a specialist.

His tones were cordial as he greeted me; "Hello, Mae, I heard you aren't feeling well, so I came all the way down here to see if I can help you." He clasped my cold, white hand in his large one. As he stroked his neat white goatee, his keen gray eyes were dictating information for the prognosis.

I was very tense as he began the examination. Gentle but with a professional thoroughness he listened, looked and tapped, making notes as he moved along. He returned his instruments and notes to his satchel and moved his chair a bit closer to my bed. His x-ray eyes were riveted on mine. I found this very disturbing. Was he able to perceive the secrets of my heart? Could he hear the silent scream?

Moments passed — long, loud moments — before he spoke. His trained finger rested lightly on the pulsating blue thread above my wrist. The strength from his hands seemed to flow through mine, warming the blood in my veins. A serious expression crossed his face, then in a low voice he asked, "Why do you fight life? You have so much to live for. Your Maker has given you talents that many would covet; yet you are letting them go to waste. How long has it been since you have painted a picture or created something new? My father was a minister, and he taught me it was wrong not to utilize the talents God has given us. What about you?"

After these words he waited quietly, letting them penetrate

beyond the surface of my mind.

Strangely enough, my mind was unusually clear and I caught his message. I felt both angry and guilty. I wondered if he knew how much it offended me. Closing my eyes did not block out his searching look. My eyes reluctantly met his. His were kind and encouraging, while hot, salty tears were flooding mine.

Words in my head were like trapped victims at an exit. Choked with emotion and almost incoherent, I gasped . . .

"Dr. Abbit, don't you understand . . . ? There is nothing for me to live for . . . I'm . . . I'm a hopeless case! I know my time is near . . . and I welcome it."

He spoke in a firm voice. "You may welcome escape, but death I'm not so sure. What about your family and friends who love you? Is it not selfish to hurt them?

"God says He alone has the right to terminate life. Do you realize you are willingly taking your own life?"

Surely I didn't hear him correctly. Am I adding suicide to my long list of sins? No, this was not suicide in my case. Dr. Abbit simply did not understand—could he not see how desperately I wanted help? How I wanted someone to cover my sins, someone to help me out of this awful whirlpool that was dragging me into its depths?

Panic seized me—the room became close and stuffy; the loud, wild drums in my ears and breast were unbearable. Slowly I began to slip into blackness. Its eddy sucked me into oblivion. Minutes slipped by.

Then the essence of aromatics was strong, and I heard, "Take a deep breath, Mae." Obeying and breathing deeply, I soon regained consciousness. Restoring his hypodermic needle to its case, Dr. Abbit returned to my side.

I realized now I had not escaped this confrontation with truth, as I heard . . .

"You realize I came to help you, but I must have your cooperation, too. I granted you a special favor by coming down here to help you, now I want you to do a favor for me.

"I want you to promise me you will make every effort to get well, to eat; start with a little food and increase it daily until you are eating normally again. Will you do this just for me?

"You must practice positive thinking by believing you are improving every day. Now, how about your answer?"

After that pointed question, he waited expectantly. The needle he gave me untied the knots in my muscles. With a lucid mind I felt the significance of these moments. His silence clamored for an answer. I realized it was futile to hide anything from him. He knew my intrinsic nature. My defenses were weakening.

How could I get beyond the high wall that had imprisoned me so long? Countless times in the past I had tried to climb over those walls, to hack through them, to squeeze under them, but all my efforts were in vain. Could he not understand it was my soul that needed help? Physical weakness I could accept, but the mental torture was a private hell to me.

I recalled how Mother in her illness saw a myriad of angels descend to bless her, and I had to battle evil imaginations.

Dr. Abbit's words were to be respected, they were not simply a lot of professional jargon. They were kind, sincere and laced with knowledge. I was deeply grateful for his concern. Somehow it gave me a measure of comfort to know that he cared.

I reasoned, "If I tell him that I do not wish to get well, I will appear so ungrateful." And I really wanted to please him, because he was so kind to me. "On the other hand, if I make this promise I will have to lie." Once more I was trapped! My convictions, like little birds, fluttered away with the truth.

Gathering the remaining remnants of integrity, I thinly stumbled through these words: "I . . . I do appreciate all you have done for me, Dr. Abbit. Just having you here has made me better already." There was a measure of truth in this; nevertheless, I knew deep down inside of me that I would not change my mind—not even for him.

"Yes, I know you appreciate my interest. But I want a direct promise from you," he replied.

My seared conscience once again burned painfully. I loathed lying . . . yet I heard my voice say, "I will eat, for your sake. I will try and get well."

"That's what I want to hear, Mae. Now, for the present you must practice positive thinking, using the methods I suggested earlier."

He remained for some time, explaining ways to overcome fears, anxieties and depression, ways to learn to accept one's self. He concluded his instructions with this profound statement: "Continue to read your Bible and pray. After all, the Great Creator made us, and He can do more for us than anyone. He cares for you."

"Hu-m-m," I chided silently, "if God cares, it takes Him a long time to show it."

Dr. Abbit rose to leave. He quickly scribbled some prescriptions and handed them to me, adding, "Don't disappoint me, Mae; I'm counting on your word. Oh, yes, I want that snow scene for my office as soon as you can get it done."

My friend was waiting patiently for the doctor on the porch. The ensuing conversation revealed that my condition was serious, both physical and mental. Also, it was evident that I needed to be hospitalized, but he concluded, "If Mae keeps her promise, she has every chance to live." He also promised to call again in a few days.

Myles returned home around five-thirty. His face mirrored his concern as he approached me. It was obvious that he had been informed and knew about Dr. Abbit's report.

Before he could speak, I pleadingly whimpered, "Please, don't make me go to the hospital. I'll do whatever you suggest, but don't make me go."

Myles disliked hospitals; even to visit others made him sick. He took his time as he contemplated the wisdom of such a decision. He seemed reluctant to commit himself. Turning to me slowly, he said, "I have learned that doctors do not have all the answers. I want more time to think it over. If you do not show any improvement soon, you will have to go for forced feeding. You can get out of all this if you make up your mind."

With that emphatic remark, he returned to the kitchen. This was not the first time I had heard those words from him.

Chapter 29

A Saintly Visitor

August's apricot sun slowly set, glowing like a molten pot of fire. She lavishly poured her warmth over our little village. Here on South Main Street we saw her golden days lined with dark shadows.

There was tension in our home and anxiety as my family watched my weakening condition. Because the doctor had advised that I should not be left alone, my family made every effort to have someone stay with me. This was not always an easy arrangement, but most of the time someone was able to be with me. Sometimes this annoyed me while other times I welcomed the company.

The dear little grandmother next door would frequently peep in to check on me. Since there was only a hall that separated our homes, that was not too difficult for her. She would bring goodies to tempt my appetite and always some loving motherly words of comfort interspersed with Bible verses.

Daddy had postponed his trip to Florida so he could be with me. Long hours he would sit by my sofa reading, sometimes aloud or more often silently. He was an avid reader, but he always read the obituary list in his newspaper first, then moved on to other items. If there was anyone in that list he knew, he was faithful to show "his respect" to the bereaved ones.

In spite of my determination to "make an exit" I was much depressed to see the sad expression on his kindly face. He had an imploring look of "please, Mae, don't give up."

Although Dad was informed by other members of the family that I purposefully was fighting every means to improve, he still found it hard to accept. It was touching to feel his love and know he cared. With all this tender manifestation, I still hardened my heart by lying daily and pretending I was better.

With each day I grew weaker. The milk and fruit juices that were served to me I deceitfully fed to the plants on the nearby window. If my family knew this, they said nothing to me.

I knew I must act fast. Three days ago Dr. Abbit had been here. That same evening Myles had challenged me to make some improvement or I would land in the hospital again.

Thursday came all too soon. Myles had the afternoon off, and after finishing his lunch he came into the living room, pulled out his favorite magazine from the rack and seated himself in a comfortable chair.

From my position in the corner at the head end of the sofa I could not see him. Nor did I maneuver myself so I could. But his smoking habit made his presence unmistakable. Somehow I knew he was not reading, but staring at me. I was motionless outwardly, silently waiting for the awful verdict that would be forthcoming.

Then it came—like a condemning stroke of doom. "It appears to me," he said in no uncertain terms, "you have made no improvement at all. I doubt if you really tried. Friday night I will call the doctor and tell him to make arrangements for your admission to the hospital." In a tone of finality he added, "This is about all I can take!"

THUMP . . . THUMP . . . THUMP . . . each heartbeat was suffocatingly loud. A binding tightness gripped my chest. My mouth felt cottony. Everything in the room blurred into a misty whiteness . . . then came total blackness.

Once again through a strange stillness came the familiar thud of my heart. This time it skipped lightly, then paused taking off again in the most erratic way.

Iced water was touching my lips. Myles was supporting my head and shoulders and encouraging me to drink. His voice was kind, and his touch was gentle. When he saw I had revived, he released me and left the room without a word. His patience was spent, and he was headed for his usual long trek in the country where he claimed he "could think things through."

Exhausted, I fell into a deep sleep and was unaware of Daddy's presence. He had made his appearance shortly after

115

Myles left and remained until five-thirty p.m. It was around seven when I awakened. The family had finished their evening meal, and my niece was practicing her piano lessons.

Suddenly I was startled by the clear notes from the front doorbell. "Bing, bong"—the staccato notes could be heard throughout the house. Their tones suggested to me that someone may be coming to visit me. In these past weeks numerous pastors and Christian friends would stop and visit.

My niece ran to open the door and I heard her say, "Yes, she is here, on the sofa, come on in."

The living room was rather dark, and it was difficult for me to recognize the person who had stepped into the room. After turning a light on, my niece left the visitor and me to ourselves.

Squinting from the sudden light, I focused my eyes and could hardly believe what I saw. Kathryn's friend from Florida was bending over me. Her warm hands clasped mine, and she whispered, "It's Marion." Her face wore the brightest smile. Her deep dimples did not dominate the features of her face as in her teen years, rather they were softened by new lines of dignity and maturity. A thick crown of braids encircled her head, and a few ringlets fell loosely about her ears and neck. Her hair, once a rich chestnut brown, was streaked with gray. Even an additional fifteen years did not remove a certain girlishness which was hers.

There was something uniquely different about her. She seemed to emanate an inner glow, a strength and a quietness that came from within. Even in my languishing state, I was keenly aware of "a presence" rather than a person. It took me back to the days of my childhood when I visited with Brother J. H. Moore in Sebring.

"Marion Roth!" I gasped in surprise. Then I remembered her last letter had said, "I will try to visit you in the near future." Recalling the contents of her letter, I began to feel uneasy. She had come to force that Holy Spirit stuff on me. I was in no mood for confusing subjects; besides, I always avoided subjects on religion in the presence of my family.

In a soft voice she began, "Mae, I guess you received my letter? I'm sure Kitty told you I was led to pray in a very special way for you. God made it clear to me that you needed help, that I am to come to your home tonight . . . so that you won't do anything desperate and leave this world unsaved."

Inside I wondered, "How did she know what I had planned to do? I had told no one." I heard the kitchen door close quietly, and I knew that my family had left for the evening; there was no one to interrupt this dreaded conversation. On the surface I was politely attentive as I listened to her explain the plan of salvation from the Bible.

I recalled she had witnessed my baptism down by the lake shore in Sebring, so what was she getting at? I simply couldn't swallow all she was saying; my mind was too weary. But one question stood out loud and clear. "Where are you going after you die?" "Marion," I whispered, "doesn't God forgive sins?"

"Yes," she said, "but only if you have put your faith in His Son who died for our sins. If we have received Jesus into our hearts we do not continue on in our sins, because the Holy Spirit indwells us. He cannot live within a sinner's heart . . . "

Interrupting her, I heard myself saying, "Oh, no, let's not talk about that Holy Spirit stuff. I'm too tired and I really don't understand."

Like a knife wound she replied, "Then you will never see your mother again! Your beautiful mother was a shining witness of Christ and the indwelling Spirit—this very same Spirit of whom you are afraid and want no part of. Mae, listen carefully as I read what the Bible says—speaking for Christ Himself who is the Word." Reading from Romans 8, she emphasized several verses, pointing out the Spirit's work and presence in a true believer. "Verse 9—'If any man have not the Spirit of Christ, he is none of His.' Verse 16—'The Spirit beareth witness with our spirit that we are the children of God.'" Her soft voice continued on reading and explaining. Much of it bypassed me, but not all. Beyond the dulled mind, like a laser beam into my very soul, deep into the recesses came a gentle tugging, a wooing of the heart like never before.

Ah, this gentle, gentle One was melting, probing, pleading, yearning within. I could not swallow for the lump in my throat, and neither could I weep.

Marion was aware of my weariness, my confusion and my inability to comprehend all that was shared with me. At the

117

same time her keen spiritual perception and her sympathetic concern for me prompted her to boldly pierce the wall within and expose the truth. "This is your trouble, Mae, simply your own sinful self. You cannot deliver yourself. I know; I too struggled like you. But Jesus freed me. He has the answer. He can free you. Do you believe that? You do not free yourself by dying—for life goes on after death. But Christ can deliver you even today if you'll let Him."

She did not even name the sins that I could not name or face. We both knew just what she meant. Her own experience to find victory and peace was a traumatic one. She claimed she had a spiritual heart transplant. Christ surely changed her life.

Then we heard the key turn in the back door; we knew my family returned and our visit must end. She concluded with a prayer and lingered only long enough to remind me about a forthcoming telegram; I also would be given a letter with instructions. Bending over me, she kissed me and left.

I knew what the letter would contain—a five-point way to deliverance and victory. I also knew she had promised to pray with others for me in great faith, believing a transformation would take place in my life as I carefully followed the enclosed instructions.

Marion's understanding and insight to my problems caused me to search my heart. One fact that bothered me most was, since she knew I was such a gross sinner, why didn't she condemn me? I looked and waited for it. Instead, she seemed to enfold me in her love.

This saintly lady learned from me that I had smoked, that I loved liquor, that I drank it whenever I could, and that evil thoughts and habits continuously hounded me. She knew I was enslaved to drugs and could not face day or night without them. Yet her faith remained unchanged in what God could do for me.

It was midnight now. Grandmother's chime clock next door told me so as its melody filtered through the walls. The street light prevented my room from total darkness. When dreams tormented me, I would open my eyes and be comforted by the sight of familiar things.

Once more the war was waging within. How can words

118

describe the soul's conflict? The Word had entered my heart, and Satan was not about to move out without a battle. The grotesque figures that paraded the halls of my mind were relentless. Their ugly accusing eyes and lecherous lips made me want to scream for help. It was as if they sneered and hawkishly laughed at me.

This night my medication would not numb my nerves and quiet my conscious thoughts. Prickles jabbed at my spine, my hands and feet felt clammy. Automatically I reached for medication. My hand shook as I fingered the bottles, then I remembered . . . "Tomorrow's the day I must use all of it. I'd better go light on it tonight." Rechecking the supply I decided to take paraldehyde tonight. It was a comforting kind of medication, if one did not object to the side effects. I reeked of the stuff. My breath, skin, even my clothes exuded a sweetish etherized scent that reminded one of embalming fluid. It was not long before I was in a soporific sleep.

Chapter 30

The Screams Grow Louder

Friday I awakened with such severe fatigue I could barely move. My body was so weak and emaciated that bathroom necessities were impossible for me to perform alone. My last weight record was seventy-two pounds, and I knew it had dropped since then. My vision blurred with every move and nausea accompanied it. I longed to slip back into a deep sleep again but my nerves were too tense.

The early morning sun flooded my room, sweeping all the shadows under the furniture.

Usually Daddy came at seven-thirty, but he had called last night and reported he had a cold and would not be able to come; was this supposed to be?

When Grandmother, next door, learned of this she offered to keep her eye on me. She never visited long, but would faithfully peep in at me every hour or so. She made her first appearance about eight o'clock bringing a cup of hot mint tea. Its fragrance pervaded throughout the room, enticing my dulled appetite. My starved body was screaming for food, and I yielded. As she held the cup to my lips I took small sips, savoring each one carefully. The fresh mint flavor was overwhelmingly pleasant held so close to my nose. It was comforting and healing as it trickled down my throat warming my stomach and renewing my strength.

It took all my strength to sip a small amount of tea. I was exhausted. She set the cup down and tried to make me more comfortable. She tucked pillows under my head and straightened the covers, then she turned to go. "I'll be back about ten o'clock after the mailman comes," she said, as she quietly closed the door.

After the tea, my mind cleared a bit more. "Why did I drink that tea today of all days! Was this not my last day? I was fasting, and now I had broken my fast." I had to admit I felt a little stronger. Glancing at my medicine I was reassured; it was all there, and enough.

It was medication time — so I helped myself to a triple dose and settled back. One thing I realized was that I must hurry. I had no intentions to go back to the hospital nor had I a mind to be forced to live.

Despite the enforced freedom from reality, nevertheless probing thoughts still nagged at my conscience. Rationalizing, I told myself it was a Christian custom to fast. "Doesn't the Bible advocate fasting?" It also was easy for me to say, "Besides, I read that by fasting one could rid one's self of the evil in the soul as well as poisons in the body." (Although I truly doubted this.) "Am I not just a burden and a care to my family anyway?"

By this time I was not aware of any physical discomfort nor could I feel a real concern about my family's reactions. In this state I imagined myself loosened from them and my surroundings. Soon I believed I would slip away. To justify my behavior I used the following reasons: Kathryn's family was large enough to keep her busy. With one on the way, she would not take it so hard after I am gone. With Daddy I was more troubled, because he had lost Mother and was hurt so deeply. But with Mother it was different, she wanted to live.

"No," I said, "I must harden my heart and go through with it. Daddy would go to Florida and would soon forget." I could just see my doctors shake their heads and say, "Mae should have been in the hospital."

In spite of the medication and my determination, there was an opposing force prodding my mind like little forks that stab with questions. "After death, what then? I may be escaping a painful world, but what about God? Marion Roth said, 'God is a Judge as well as a Justifier.'"

"Oh, God," I implored, "bear with me and understand there seems no other way out . . . quickly take me away!"

Again Marion's words returned to my mind. "You cannot meet your mother if you leave this world unsaved."

"Mother," I pleaded, "Dear Mother, please forgive me, I do not purposefully want to hurt you. If only I could come to you now."

Suppose she was correct, how could I bear not seeing Mother again. These doubts were tormenting my mind . . . Shivering, I turned on my side and pulled the covers up closer to my chin.

Something was strange about these moments. What was it that made me feel a strong sense of opposition and conflict? I had made up my mind to end it all — that was final . . . so why the conflict . . . the doubts?

The usual amount of medication would have put me to sleep by now, but I had tripled it and I seemed more aware of my situation than ever.

I could not sink into oblivion, nor could I quiet down. If only I could SLAM the door SHUT! The SCREAMS were growing LOUDer.

I heard my voice whisper, "Is now the time for all of it? Right now?"

The room silently held my words as if waiting . . .

"No, I must take the medication carefully and in timed doses. There is less chance of violent vomiting and convulsions," or so I had read somewhere. I was counting on going into a deep permanent sleep.

My eyes stared at the drug supply on the nearby end table. It was comforting to see it was all there. At eleven I would take my second large dose. I decided to wait until then.

I was surprised to discover a letter propped between my glass and a book. Welcoming anything that would divert my troubled thoughts, I leaned over and picked it up. The handwriting was Marion's, and it was addressed to me. She had placed it there knowing I would find it. I slowly began to read:

Dear Mae:

Please read this carefully. Within is the solution to all your problems. I know you are not really ready to die. Several of my friends are claiming God's promises for you. And He can and will heal you if you will let Him. You have tried everything else and found it all a failure — now try Him. Please give Him a chance and see what He will do for you. Jesus Christ is the answer.

Enclosed was a direct and simple method to come to the Lord.

She informed me that at ten I would receive a telegram; this would contain brief instructions on how to come to Christ.

At that same hour in New Jersey, a prayer meeting would be in session. They would specifically pray that I would be saved and be filled with His Holy Spirit.

Marion advised me not to expect an exciting experience or look for some unusual happening. I was told to come to the Lord alone and just as I was. God would move and work in my life as He saw fit.

When one comes alone before Him one can talk aloud, pouring out one's heart to Him. I was to name every known sin, past and present, that I had committed. Since I had so little faith I was to confess this too, expecting Him to intercede for me in my unstable state.

After I had sincerely followed all the rules I was to praise and thank Him (no matter how I felt) for what He would do for me.

Marion's instructions were easy to follow. All were on the positive side. Remembering the influence of medication, she used scripture sparingly. It was made clear that Salvation was a free Gift — never to be earned, but given to all who accepted Jesus Christ as their Saviour.

Here was a simple and direct way to invite Christ into my heart, to find the answers to all of my problems, to once and for all be delivered and find true Peace.

1. *How to take Christ as your Saviour.* (John 3:16)
   Lord Jesus, I am a lost sinner, will you come into my heart and save me? Praise and thank Him right now, no matter what!

2. *How to receive forgiveness and cleansing.* (John 1:7)
   I believe you died for my sins. Forgive me and wash me — make me whiter than snow.

3. *How to receive the Holy Spirit.*
   Ye shall receive power . . . (Acts 1:8). Ask anything in my name . . . Lord Jesus fill me with your Holy Spirit (John 14:14). Ye were sealed with the Holy Spirit of promise — (Eph. 1:13).

4. *How to be sure I am saved and filled with His Spirit.* (John 4:13, 5:13)

   Whosoever calleth on the name of the Lord shall be saved. I will rely on the faithfulness of God and His Word. I will have changed attitudes and desires.

5. *How to live victoriously.* (I Thes. 5:23, Phil. 4:13, II Cor. 2:14)

   I can do *all* things through Christ who strengthens me. Thanks be unto God who *always* causeth us to triumph in Christ.

Chapter 31

The Glory Spell . . . And More!

Numerous doubts assailed me as I slowly read her letter. Besides the doubts came yearnings, too. I longed for the peace and freedom Marion said could be mine.

The enemy of the human heart is cunning and clever. His persuasions are strong. The control he had over me was great. His accusations were subtle, and he amplified my fears. "Marion has never been in your shoes," he argued. "How can she prove you can be healed, haven't all your past efforts been useless? I would not take her words too seriously . . . " and so on. My defenses were tottering as he kept up his barrage.

Soon the conflict intensified; my muscles knotted, and I began to grow cold and stiff. An eerie darkness crept around until I could feel its breath. Was I being transported . . . but where . . . ? Suddenly my eyes were looking beyond the room and the walls and peering into another world. Unfolding before me was a deep chasm. I was precariously balanced on its edge. My toes were tightly gripping the crumbling ledge. Suddenly there was a thick splitting sound behind me as the rock and the earth divided.

Standing there on the trembling rock, I knew in a moment I'd be hurled into the abyss below. Slowly it tore away from its setting and I plunged forward. I could feel the pull of my body as it sank into the deep below.

In these fleeting moments a profile of my life passed before me — twenty-six years of life recorded in eternity. There was no time to repent or restore the lost years. In despair I wept as I saw the futility of it all. "If only . . . if only . . . I could have another chance!" Great pulsations throbbed throughout my body. Each one was a total cry for help.

The whirling, suffocating descent was endless. Then beyond all this agony, like a silvery voice heard in a seashell, my name was called. Not once but three times.

With barely a thread of strength I reached out for the call. More clearly now I heard, "Mae, Mae, are you all right?" A wave of relief swept over me as I realized the panorama of horror had vanished.

Little Grandmother was anxiously bending over me, rubbing my forehead and hands. "Did you have a bad dream? I vas ready to call the doctor vhen I couldn't avaken you." As she continued her questions, I began to respond. "Are you sure you didn't take too much medicine?"

"I'm all right," I feebly tried to assure her. "What an awful dream I had!" She gently bathed my face and offered me a drink of cool water, then seated herself beside me.

She quietly studied my face for a time, then breaking the silence she asked, "Are you able to read now?" Not waiting for an answer, she took a yellow envelope from her apron and handed it to me.

"It's a telegram for you; must be something special." It was indeed something special, although I did not realize it then.

The opaque veil was lifting and once more I was able to concentrate. When Grandma observed that I showed interest in the telegraph, she commented. "Vell, I guess you're all right now. I'll be back shortly to check on you." I smiled a "thank you" as she closed the door. Opening the envelope, I found the enclosed message.

PRAYER MEETING 10:00 a.m. for you STOP Go to Jesus alone STOP If Unable to Pray read this aloud to him STOP
REPEAT FOLLOWING STOP
   1. Jesus come into my heart STOP
   2. I am a sinner STOP confess all sins STOP
   3. Fill me with the Holy Spirit STOP
   4. Thank you, Lord STOP
Sing any praise hymn you know STOP He is able STOP Your prayer Warriors STOP

Having read the telegram, I folded it and carefully tucked it under my nightie, right over my heart. There was much to consider, and I must order my thoughts. It was almost 10 a.m.

The mailman would be here soon, and Grandma would bring it right over to me. If she saw that I was back to normal, she would not check again for another hour or two.

Lying there, quietly waiting for her to bring the mail, I began to realize I had reached a climactic point in my life. Having just come through the previous experience of seeing my life hurled into a dark unknown chaos, it was impossible to ignore the letter or the telegram. I was unable to reason clearly, nevertheless I was aware that within their contents was the answer—the answer to my cry. God was the one I must rely on. Suddenly I realized that I was not afraid. There was no need to keep running. Although I was completely alone, I sensed a warm and comforting Presence in the room. Something vaguely encouraging me.

To this day I am unable to explain that indefinable Presence. Could it have been a ministering angel? Where had the urgency and determination to die gone? Why was I stirred within the recesses of my being to turn to God?

Marion had said folks were praying. Were the powers of darkness restrained through their prayers? At that time I could not explain the spiritual essence that pervaded my room, but it was surely there.

Another amazing thing occurred to me. I no longer derived satisfaction from the thoughts of death. Instead, a tender yearning stirred within.

Footsteps in the hall announced Grandmother was collecting the mail and would bring our mail over shortly. In no time at all she placed the mail on the table, commented that I appeared brighter, replaced my glass with fresh water, then added hurriedly, "Pop vants his lunch before noon, so I'll come over between twelve-thirty and one o'clock. You better try to rest avhile now." Before the door closed I knew what I was going to do.

I pushed my covers back, got up from the sofa, pulled my robe about me and headed for the stairway. Lightheaded and weak, I waited to catch my breath, then I managed to open the door.

Emaciated as I was, it was impossible to walk alone, but at this point I did not question how I would get upstairs. In a sitting position I worked my body up on each step, panting, and puffing, until I reached the top.

My body was energized by an unseen force. I was motivated by one thought, "I need help." Did not the note say 'Jesus was able'? As a last resource I would turn to Him.

Every nerve in my body was quivering as I pushed myself across the floor to the side of my bed. A knife-like pain gripped my chest and moved into my throat; my skin was cool and moist as I limply laid across the edge of the bed and waited for the pain to subside. Then I became aware of the envelope tucked near to my heart. I remembered why it was important to me. Spreading it before me, I began to read. With a clear mind I could comprehend the printed message; but I was totally empty emotionally. There was no eager anticipation, no hope, only an indefinable panting for God. I was not conscious of a grain of faith. "Had I not prayed before and begged for help?" So here I was on my trembling knees, waiting . . . .

Marion's note said, "Go alone and place the paper before you." I had followed her instructions so far.

"What could I tell God that was different than what I had said before?" Dulled by medication, and feeling completely helpless, I decided to read the telegram out loud. Weakly, I repeated, "Jesus, come into my heart." (My letter said, "Don't expect anything to happen. If you have no faith, tell God about that, too.") After a moment I added, "I have no faith, God, so you'll have to take care of that, too."

Glancing at the telegram before me, I decided to repeat point two. My voice sounded strange as though it were mocking as I repeated, "I am a sinner," adding, "confess all your sins." She had reminded me during our visit and in her letter I was to confess all my sins. All my sins? How could I recall them all — or reveal them in sordid detail to God?

As I began to confess some sins that I hated in myself, others surfaced so fast that I could not sort them out. "God," I said, "I feel like I am exposing the most awful things to You." On and on they poured from my lips, sins from way back in my childhood days.

I had harbored lies, envyings, cheatings, deceptions,

jealousies and deep hidden resentments. Murder, too, I was guilty of. (Wasn't wishing someone out of the way, murder?) Once I killed a helpless turtle, and it troubled my conscience all through my childhood. I stole some pennies from Mother's pocketbook and accepted money that did not belong to me. The secret sins were the worst of all: lustful thoughts and desires like adultery and fornication. Out poured the filth and stench of fleshly indulgences — some that hurt others, but not nearly as much as they hurt me. I was humiliated and so ashamed of these horrible sins as I exposed them to a Holy God who knew all about them.

As I continued to confess, naming sins as sins, not calling them shortcomings, misdeeds and the like, I became aware of a feeling of freedom, a release as though a tremendous burden was lifting. There was a spirit of contrition and repentance that I had never known before. Kneeling before the Almighty God who is my Judge, the words from Jeremiah 17:9, "The heart is deceitful above all things and desperately wicked, who can know it?," portrayed my hopeless condition.

Broken and waiting before Him, the flood gates of my heart overflowed. Sobs shook my frail body as I wept.

Ah, but this Holy One I feared so much had a deeper work to perform in my waiting heart. Presently a voice was heard saying, "You are not quite emptied, Mae."

I replied, weeping, "What have I withheld, Lord?" In this soul-searching silence He left me to dwell; He would not compel me, I must come with my will.

There is no halfway with God. He not only wanted to remove my sins, but He wanted me. This was difficult to understand. After standing before Him stripped of every pretense, having confessed all my sins, what was there left to offer Him?

I was slowly led to see the source of my trouble. It was SELF. In its most subtle and delicate way it evaded my mind of its need to be brought to the Lord. "But surely, Lord," I said, "You don't need this part of me; are there no rights left to a person at all?" The tear-soaked coverlet absorbed my sobs as I buried my face in it, knowing full well He must have SELF, too.

In my tender years I had learned that Christ died on the cross and shed his blood for our sins. But at this moment I saw Him as MY suffering Saviour who died in MY place and for MY sins.

In great sorrow I wept anew for His anguish. What unspeakable love He had for me! Now I needed no direction to speak and pray to my Lord. Broken in spirit I prayed, "Lord Jesus, I bring myself to You, do with me what you will." Following this commitment, I praised and thanked Him.

Even today as I share these awesome moments, my eyes are filled with tears, and I must fall on my knees before Him for I am on hallowed ground. God met me in an unspeakable way. Only the Holy Spirit can reveal the meaning and reality of this experience.

A phenomenal perception was imparted to me. I was kneeling in the center of a flowing fountain. The heart of this fountain appeared as a crimson stream. I felt its cleansing power flow through my veins, purging and purifying my innermost being. The outer flow of the fountain was transparently pure and radiant. I could scarcely breathe for the tremendous strength of this efficacious power that was flooding my spirit. Hushed in these wondrous moments, I knew I was being bathed in the Spirit . . . to behold the face of my wonderful Lord.

With anointed eyes I saw this Infinite One whose holiness exceeds the brightness of the sun, and for moments I was struck dumb.

Then a rapturous joy flooded my soul in so great a measure I could only whisper, "It is enough, it is enough. I cannot bear any more!" There just wasn't enough room to contain it all! Such unrestrained joy found ways of expression in utterances of praise as I've never been able to repeat again. My head was raised and my arms upheld as my entire person burst forth in song.

There is a fountain filled with blood
Drawn from Immanuel's veins,
And sinners plunged beneath that flood
Lose all their guilty stains.

The dying thief rejoiced to see
that fountain in his day
And there may I, though vile as he,
Wash all my sins away.

E'er since by faith I saw the stream
Thy flowing wounds supply,
Redeeming love (is now) my theme
And shall be till I die, and shall be till I die . . .

W. Cowper

Once more I was mindful of my human frame as I knelt there beside my bed. The tear-soaked telegram was forgotten.

Gone was the defeated and dying Mae. I was a new creature in Christ. I had personally witnessed my own liberation from sin, and before I could ask, God had graciously filled me with the Holy Spirit.

Charged with a new strength I rose to my feet and made my way downstairs and out to the kitchen. Opening the refrigerator, I helped myself to a small glass of milk (to drink, not to pour on the plants!). Returning to the sofa I slowly sipped until the glass was empty. It did not matter that salty tears of joy were flavoring the milk. My deep joy was overflowing, and I couldn't wait to tell someone. If only Grandma would come, she would understand.

A glance at the clock revealed that it was two-thirty. "Had Grandma forgotten? Not finding me on the sofa-bed would surely upset her." It wasn't long before I heard her hurrying across the hall. Hopeful that I'd be sleeping, she quietly entered the room.

She took one look at me and exclaimed, "Vhy, Mae! Vot hoppened, you look so bright, your face chust shines!" As she came closer and stared, the little furrows multiplied on her brow in amazement.

"You are sitting up, and drinking some milk, vonce now!" she exclaimed.

"Please sit down, Grandmother. I must talk to someone or I'll burst."

"I took a nap," she interjected, "and overslept. Vas

somebody here to make you so happy?"

"No, Grandmother, it's just that I saw Jesus—really saw Him, and the Holy Spirit came into my life to live! I am going to get well, do you understand? I'm going to get well!"

"Och, vell, that's vonderful, I guess you had a 'glory spell.'" Leaning over me, she kissed me, adding, "Praise the Lord, our prayers are answered." Her face was all smiles as she hurried across the hall to tell Pop.

Yes, I had a "glory spell" and much more. Such an amazing transformation had taken place in my spirit, soul and body. Miracle upon miracles happened. Unbelievable things were experienced as God continued to work in my life.

From these glorious moments to several decades later, Jesus has become dearer to me than words can tell.

God moves in mysterious ways and His way with me was unique indeed. I never dreamed I would be able to minister to hundreds, much less to seven very special people—my beloved family.

Two books could not hold the exciting ways God has worked in my life. If He continues to lengthen my days, to inspire my mind and heart, I shall joyfully allow my pen to be a ready witness for Him.

"For those who think the high rate of divorce is simply a product of the times and there's not much we can do about it, this slim volume provides a great deal of hope. There <u>are</u> answers, and Michael McManus in *Insuring Marriage: 25 Proven Ways to Prevent Divorce* presents them in the form of fresh stories of actual experiences. This book should be read by those considering marriage, those thinking about ending their marriages, and even those who want their marriage to remain happy and intact."

George H. Gallup, Jr.
Gallup International Institute

"The church can no longer turn its back on the problem of divorce. I am encouraged to see, at last, resources that meet this problem head on with valuable, workable solutions that are already making a difference. It is now possible, with these tested and effective methods, to stop the relentless tide of divorce once and for all. Mike McManus' *Marriage Savers* resources need to find their way into every church around the world."

Dr. Jimmy Draper, President
Baptist Sunday School Board

"Too many people get divorced far too easily. Michael McManus gives solid practical advice on how to avoid divorce. It is the kind of advice that is biblically sound but devoid of worn out pieties. This is good stuff."

Tony Campolo, Writer/Speaker

"I am delighted to do all that I can to encourage 'Marriage Savers' and think this absolutely must be a very, very high priority."

The Most Rev. William H. Keeler
President, National Conference
of Catholic Bishops

Insuring
Marriage

25 PROVEN WAYS
TO PREVENT DIVORCE

MICHAEL J. McMANUS

LifeWay Press
Nashville, Tennessee

7800-01

ISBN: 0-8054-9878-8

Dewey Decimal Classification 306.81
Subject Heading: Marriage/Domestic Relations

Unless indicated otherwise, Scripture
quotations are from the Holy Bible,
New International Version,
copyright © 1973, 1978, 1984
by International Bible Society.

Printed in the United States of America

LifeWay Press
127 Ninth Avenue, North
Nashville, Tennessee 37234

Dedicated
to couples whose marriages
have been joyous,
growing experiences for decades,
who have a heart to serve as mentors
to the seriously dating, engaged,
or newlyweds, or perhaps
to those in deeply troubled marriages
and to pastors who will
"prepare God's people for works of service,"
as marriage savers.

Acknowledgments

I would never have written this book if it were not for Harriet, my wife and best friend for nearly three decades. She has added so much joy to my life, and our marriage grew so profoundly through our Marriage Encounter weekend that I developed an interest in other ways to save or strengthen marriages. She has also been the more active partner of our work as a mentor couple in working with seriously dating and engaged couples and in training other mentors.

I'm grateful to the 100+ newspapers which first published many of these "answers" on how to avoid divorce in my nationally syndicated column, "Ethics and Religion." I also want to thank Zondervan for publishing my first book, *Marriage Savers,* which has sparked a movement within denominations and communities to do a better job preparing couples for marriage and sustaining existing ones.

One of the first people to read *Marriage Savers* and see its potential was Dr. Jimmy Draper, President of the Baptist Sunday School Board. He was the first national religious leader to recognize the many practical ways that churches could become "marriage savers." He also saw the importance of producing materials that could help other denominations preserve marriages.

I also want to express my appreciation to Joe Musser, the producer of six "Marriage Saver Videos" that make these answers come alive, who in his spare time, also contributed to this book.

Finally, I want to thank **you** for buying this book. My prayer is that it will help you build a lifelong marriage.

Michael J. McManus
October 1994

FOREWORD

Christians are reading the news these days and rubbing their eyes in amazement. Suddenly the world seems to be waking up to the crucial role morality plays in public policy.

First the sophisticated *Atlantic Monthly* magazine startled readers with an article announcing "Dan Quayle Was Right" showing the harm that children suffer from family breakdown. Then the *Wall Street Journal* published an article by social scientist Charles Murray, arguing that illegitimacy is the most reliable predictor of a host of social pathologies—poverty, crime, drug abuse, and welfare dependency.

All our vaunted poverty, welfare, and drug programs have less effect, it turns out, than decisions made by individual men and women to wait for marriage and maturity before they have children. Our most pressing social problems stem from moral decisions made in the heart of family life.

This realization could mean a dramatic new openness to Christian ethics. For decades public policy was pursued as though it could ignore moral questions. But now policy makers recognize that when a society's moral sense decays—particularly in regard to the family—the center cannot hold.

For the church, this represents a remarkable opportunity. By equipping Christians for strong marriages, we can set an example, demonstrating that there are answers to society's most pressing social crisis. To be salt in a decaying society, the church must boldly preach the biblical ethics of sex and marriage. We must take a strong stance against premarital sex and cohabitation. With *Insuring Marriage: 25 Proven Ways to Prevent Divorce,* Michael McManus gives us just the tools we need for the task.

First, this book gives statistics to back up biblical teachings. For example, one study found that those who engage in premarital sexual relations are 71 percent more likely to divorce than those who remain virgins. McManus also provides statistics that identify the need to adopt biblical teachings. For example, he states that though 75 percent of American weddings are blessed by a pastor, priest, or rabbi, six out of ten new marriages will fail.

Second, churches should make use of the programs listed here to help build strong marriages. For teens, abstinence programs teach how to resist sexual temptation. For engaged couples, a premarital questionnaire can spotlight problem areas and even predict who will divorce. Married couples can attend enrichment retreats. Couples in deeply troubled marriages can participate in programs that restore their relationship.

Third, a church can avoid being a "wedding factory" by setting standards for couples that ask for a church wedding. McManus describes an exciting project called a Community Marriage Policy that has the potential of cutting a community's divorce rate.

Restoring the family is one area where the church should be taking the lead. The government can't. The media isn't. The schools aren't. You and I need to take up the task of equipping people for strong marriages. This book can be our manual for getting started.

Christians have long argued the importance of private morality in shaping public virtue. By becoming marriage savers, we can make that point dramatically—and in the process fight the most virulent cancer eating at the heart of our culture.

Charles Colson
Washington, DC, 1994

Introduction

Getting married in America has become a gamble—a losing gamble. More than half of all new marriages are failing. Are you in such a marriage? Perhaps you or those close to you have considered divorce. Or, if unmarried, are you afraid of making the wrong choice?

If so, *Insuring Marriage: 25 Proven Ways to Prevent Divorce* is for you! The basic thesis of this book is that **divorce can be prevented**. Some of you may be asking yourselves, "Why should I stay in a bad marriage?" Let me quote a respected family author and advocate:

> Don't permit the possibility of divorce to enter your thinking. Even in moments of great conflict and discouragement, divorce is no solution.[1]
>
> James Dobson

Most people assume, wrongly, that it's impossible to improve a bad marriage. Don't despair. There are answers! In fact, even marriages with serious problems can be saved.

This book offers principles for "marriage insurance" to help you prevent divorce by learning how to build a lifelong marriage. The good news is that **there is hope**.

- Bad marriages can be avoided before they begin.
- Engaged couples can be provided "marriage insurance."
- Existing marriages can be strengthened.
- Deeply troubled marriages can be saved.
- Separated couples can rebuild their marriages.
- Divorce rates can be decreased.

What's Wrong With Divorce?

Before offering suggestions on how to avoid divorce, let's consider what is wrong with divorce. Here are four major reasons to avoid divorce.

1. Scripture Speaks Against Divorce

Scripturally, divorce is condemned in both the Old and New Testaments. The Bible's position against divorce is clear. Jesus spoke against divorce (Matt. 19) and the Old Testament writer Malachi predicts three negative consequences of divorce: great sorrow; a distress that prayer can't help; and children of divorce are likely to be rebellious, not "godly offspring" (see Mal. 2:13-16). The biblical message is so hard that some pastors are reluctant to preach on it. This is a grievous disservice to their congregations who come to believe that they can divorce with the Lord's blessing.

2. Divorce Is Harmful to Children

When a child loses a parent to divorce the child is bound to be affected in some way by the loss. Karl Zinsmeister says in an article in *The American Enterprise* that there is vast scientific evidence showing that kids are the casualties when families break up in divorce. They end up with intellectual, physical, and emotional scars. He says that the drug crisis, the crisis in our schools, and the problems of teen pregnancy and juvenile crime can be traced to one predominant source—broken families, the result of divorce.

Most divorces lead to remarriage, but to different spouses. And since 60 percent of remarriages fail, the odds are that a second divorce will occur before their children reach age 18. Thus, half the children of divorce may experience a broken home more than once before they graduate from high school.

3. Poverty Is Often a Result of Divorce

Do responsible parents want their children to live in poverty? In 1991, a National Commission on Children reported that when parents divorce or separate, children are the victims. Youngsters living with one parent, usually their mothers, are six times as likely to be living at the poverty level than kids who live with both parents. Other studies confirm that kids do best when they have the attention and financial support of **both** father and mother in a stable marriage.

Only 15.5 percent of divorced mothers receive alimony—and usually only for a year or two.[2] And what about child support? Only a small fraction of divorced mothers get full child support. And "full" payments for many are not large: *$150 per month*!

4. The Pain of Divorce Continues for Adults

According to the book, *Second Chances* by Judith Wallerstein and Sandra Blakslee, in 90 percent of the cases either the former husband or wife (or both) is still in pain ten years after divorce.[3]

These findings come as a complete surprise to most Americans who believe that divorce is just another crisis to be dealt with so that the parties can "get on with their lives."

However, years after divorce, most families still suffer the anguish. Everyone in the family is wounded, angry, and most still haven't gotten their lives together. The adults of divorce have unexpected emotional and behavioral problems with their children.

A woman whose marriage ended in divorce a decade ago told me, "Divorce is like suffering death without a funeral. The pain never ends."

So, you can readily see that for everyone involved finding ways to improve a marriage is better than dissolving it.

DIVORCE IS USUALLY NO ANSWER

In certain cases couples should separate—where physical abuse, persistent alcoholism, or adultery is present. However, according to a Gallup Poll, only 5 percent of marriages are dissolved due to physical abuse; 16 percent of divorces were attributed to alcoholism; and 17 percent to adultery. The overwhelming cause of divorce is *incompatibility* (47 percent) and *arguments* over money, family or children (10 percent).[4]

In other words, nearly 60 percent of all divorces are caused by poor communication. **These are the very marriages which most easily can be saved**.

BE A MARRIAGE SAVER

The "25 Proven Ways to Prevent Divorce" in this book are treated as answers to the question, **"What can I do?"** They are written succinctly to give a quick overview of steps to prepare for marriage or to strengthen an existing marriage. Most of the "Answers" will only whet your appetite, so each concludes with suggestions on where to learn more. Two are mentioned regularly:

- *Marriage Savers*, a book packed with details on how you, your church, and community can be a marriage saver.
- *Marriage Savers Resource Collection*, a series of six videos featuring people you will read about in this book. The collection also includes a copy of this book and *Marriage Savers*.

Please don't miss the Marriage Savers Declaration at the end of this book. I hope you will sign it as an expression of your commitment to insuring marriages.

Insuring Marriage: 25 Proven Ways to Prevent Divorce is written to give you hope. My prayer for you is that you may bond with another in marriage to bring joy to your life. Then I hope you will share what you've learned and **be a marriage saver!**

Michael J. McManus

---

[1]James C. Dobson, *Love for a Lifetime*, (Portland: Multnomah Press, 1987), 103.

[2]National Commission on Children. *Beyond Rhetoric: A New American Agenda for Children and Families*. Final Report. Washington, D.C., 1991.

[3]Judith Wallerstein and Sandra Blakslee, *Second Chances*, (New York: Ticknor & Fields, 1989), XV.

[4]Michael J. McManus, *Marriage Savers*, (Grand Rapids: Zondervan, 1993), 123.

Insuring Marriage

How Can I Become a Marriage Saver?

25 Answers

Basics for Being a Marriage Saver
1. Marriage Is Vulnerable to Divorce: Heed the Warning Signs
2. Take Seriously What the Bible Says About Key Issues Related to Divorce
3. Help Your Church Insure Future Marriages

Helping Single Adults and Seriously Dating Couples
4. Help Teenagers Abstain from Sex
5. Beware of Sexual Entrapments!
6. Don't Live Together in a Trial Marriage
7. Seriously Dating Couples Can Avoid Mistakes
8. Learn From a Relationship That Doesn't Lead to Marriage

Marriage Insurance for Engaged Couples
9. Use a Premarital Inventory to Identify Strengths and Weaknesses
10. Help Insure and Save Marriages by Being a Mentor Couple
11. Participate in a Premarital Retreat to Improve Communication Skills
12. Invest Time and Energy in Marriage Preparation

Helping Couples Strengthen Their Marriage

Even Deeply Troubled Marriages Can Be Saved

Helping the Separated or Divorced and Stepfamilies

Be a Marriage Saver

Marriage Savers Declaration

A N S W E R 1

Heed the Warning Signs of a Troubled Relationship

Relationships between men and women tend to go through phases which are predictable—but always seem surprising to those involved. First, there is the glow of romance in which a beloved can do no wrong. Then comes a time of growing disillusionment when they can do nothing right!

At that point, mature people recognize that they must invest more of themselves to **build a lasting relationship.** Conversely, immature people react poorly. They whine and complain and drive the relationship toward the rocks.

In fact, the natural direction of male-female relationships in America of the 1990s is to **separate.** Centrifugal forces drive people apart. He gets involved in his work and his hobbies, and she gets involved in her work and the children. Disillusionment builds as they drift apart.

But to be forewarned is to be forearmed.

You can build a marriage relationship that will endure if you are selfless rather than selfish and if you make the Lord the third partner in the relationship. That, in a nutshell, is the message of this book. This book is packed with suggestions on how to deal with a wide range of warning signs for dating couples and the already married. The chapters are written as **Answers** for each stage of the marital life cycle beginning with teenagers, then moving to seriously dating couples, a warning to those tempted to enter a "trial marriage," giving engaged couples "marriage insurance," providing a number of ways to strengthen existing marriages and save even the most deeply troubled ones, ideas to reconcile the separated and divorced, and ending with ways to make stepfamilies successful. Answer 1 will summarize warning signs that will be discussed in the following chapters.

WARNING SIGNS OF TROUBLE

Warning signs of trouble reveal themselves at whatever your stage of life may be. Many people have an idealistic view of marriage and are often "blindsided" by the problems that lead to divorce. Newlyweds are often astounded by the conflict that comes early to their marriage. After the wedding, a period of adjustment sets in, and the charm and enchantment of dating and courtship is but a blurred recollection.

FIRST YEAR CHECKUP

If you are married, consider your first year of marriage. Check all areas that apply.

We found ourselves in regular conflict over:

___ money management
___ time with each other
___ expectations
___ his/her family
___ church involvement
___ other: _____

How many areas did you check? If you are in your first year of marriage and checked

more than one, discuss these with a counselor or your pastor. These can be warning
signs for future conflict.

Warning signs can be a signal that a relationship
may be vulnerable to separation and divorce. Many
of the warning signs could have been noticed while
couples were seriously dating or engaged.

Warning Signs for the Dating Couple
• Premature sexual involvement.

Studies show that unmarried couples who have
sex before marriage are more likely to divorce.
Conversely, virgins have a much better chance of a
lifelong marriage relationship. Here is evidence that
Paul was right when he encouraged the Corinthians
to "flee sexual immorality" (1 Cor. 6:18).

Divorce Prevention Inventory for Single Adults

___ I am single and currently engaging in
sexual intercourse with the opposite sex.

___ I am single and in a dating relationship
that has become physically intense too
soon.

If you checked either of these, consider
making a commitment to abstain from sexual
intercourse before marriage. Work on deepening your relationship as friends. Give it
time to develop.

The emphasis from our society is on convincing
young people that premarital sex is OK. This message is promoted in school, on TV, in magazines,

motion pictures, magazines, and music. Even in this day of AIDS and high rates of teen pregnancy it is rare to hear a message of sexual abstinence.

• Too much time together.

Couples who spend too much time together in a relationship, long before an engagement, may fall into the trap of too much intimacy that leads to pre-marital sex.

Dr. Jim Talley suggests couples find ways of cutting back on the time they spend alone with each other in order to protect themselves from being "too close too soon." He suggests you first build a friendship, then a marriage.

• Ignorance about the other person.

Since most people don't reveal the "warts" to the person they are trying to impress, many important aspects of a relationship are ignored until after the wedding.

As these details emerge, so do the problems. Some problems are so serious they can break a marriage apart. Reason dictates, to learn as much as possible about each other *before* the wedding.

Caution signs should go up if a seriously dating couple cannot answer the most basic questions about each other. Questions include: What is his/her family background? What is his/her social, economic, ethnic, religious, and moral background?

Couples have to feel more than just a sexual attraction for their marriage to succeed. When there are extreme differences in their backgrounds, the stage is set for potential marital mayhem.

• A lack of instruction and training.

If we want to drive a car without complications or collisions, we study driver education and take tests to prove that we have learned what we were taught.

Yet, when we come to the serious, lifelong consideration of marriage, little instruction is offered. The church can provide this training for the nearly and newly married. Many suggestions will be made for instruction throughout this book.

Warning Signs for the Married Couple

Certain signs in a marriage relationship can alert us to potential conflict and the possibility of divorce. Check the following warning signs that may apply to your relationship. Suggestions for addressing these warning signs will be provided throughout this book in the Answers that follow.

___ *The number and frequency of arguments.*

Disagreements are natural. They don't have to be ugly. There are ways to resolve conflict that are healthy and can actually strengthen a relationship. Married couples must learn how to deal constructively with conflict.

___ *The tendency of one (or both) of the spouses to be overtly critical of the other mate.* Putting down your spouse in public or in other ways destroying his/her love, intimacy, or trust eventually damages the relationship.

___ *The loss of self-confidence and assurance.* When a spouse lacks the self-confidence to demand respect from a mate, one of two things will happen—both negative. Either the weaker person will placate the bully, or the bully will lose so much respect that he or she will find someone else to respect and will push for a divorce. Also, if one of the partners shows poor self-esteem or feels ignored, abandoned, or betrayed by the other partner, serious trouble lies ahead.

___ *Financial areas.* Financial disagreements cause many of the problems in a marriage. Married couples should resolve how money will be spent.

___ *Questions concerning children can be warning signs.* Does each partner share similar ideas of family planning? Will you have children—if so, how many—and when? Will Mom (or Dad) stay home with them while the other spouse works—or will both parents work?

These warning signs cover a variety of potential problem areas that couples need to address before the situation becomes critical. Divorce is generally a decision that is arrived at over a period of time— few divorces are the result of spontaneous blow-ups.

When the warning signs begin to surface, the wise couple will find ways to deal with them in positive, constructive methods. If you checked any of the warning signs listed here, seek help through time together, counseling, a mentor couple, or group study. And continue reading the Answers in this book!

Biblical References
Matthew 7:24, 25; Ephesians 5:25, 28; Colossians 3:18, 19; 1 Peter 3:7

Other Resources
1. *Marriage Savers* by Michael McManus (Zondervan, 1993), chapters 2 and 3.

2. *Restoring a Loving Marriage* by Jay Kesler with Joe Musser (David C. Cook, 1989).

3. *Too Close Too Soon* by Jim Talley and Bobbie Reed. (Thomas Nelson, 1982) Call 1-800-645-3761 to order direct from Jim Talley.

A N S W E R   2

Insuring Marriage

Take Seriously What the Bible Says About Key Issues Related to Divorce

Since sex outside of marriage, cohabitation, and other moral and ethical problems are contributing factors to divorce, we must look to Scripture to find answers. The church can prevent divorce by upholding God's standards. Let's consider three examples, their applications, and the biblical standards.

Key Issue: Broken pledge of faithfulness
Biblical Standard: Faithfulness in marriage
Biblical Reference: Malachi 2:13-16; Matthew 19:9
Malachi's indictment on divorce extended to the people as a whole:

> You flood the Lord's altar with tears. You weep and wail because he no longer pays attention to your offerings or accepts them with pleasure from your hands. You ask, "Why?" It is because the Lord is acting as the witness between you and the wife of your youth, because you have broken faith with her, though she is your partner, the wife of your marriage covenant.

Has not the Lord made them one? In flesh and spirit they are his. And why one? Because he was seeking godly offspring. So guard yourself in your spirit, and do not break faith with the wife of your youth. "I hate divorce," says the Lord God of Israel.

Key Issue: Cohabitation
Biblical Standard: Cease cohabiting until marriage, abstain from premarital sex
Biblical References: John 4:18; 1 Corinthians 6:18; 1 Thessalonians 4:3-5

In 1993 I spoke to pastors from 16 denominations in 10 southern cities and asked them, "How many of you have preached a sermon on cohabitation?"

In city after city, not one hand went up. So I told them: "You are part of the problem. Scripture is certainly clear on this issue. In his letter to the Corinthians Paul says, 'Flee sexual immorality.' So why haven't you preached about the wrongs of cohabitation?"

Perhaps they did not know that there is *sociological evidence* of the harm of unmarried men and women living together *which supports the biblical position.* (Cohabitation and premarital sex will be discussed in detail later in this book.)

Key Issue: The church's failure to address lax moral standards
Biblical Standard: Value-based morality embraced by believers
Biblical References: Malachi 2:8; 1 Corinthians 6:9-10; 1 Thessalonians 4:3-5

The church's failure to teach about divorce is no better now than it was in fifth century B.C. Israel. Malachi 2:8 says, "But you have turned from the way and by your teaching have caused many to stumble."

About three-fourths of all first marriages are

blessed by pastors, priests, and rabbis, according to the National Center for Health Statistics. Yet six out of ten new marriages end in divorce or separation.

Thus, the church itself is part of the divorce problem. Clearly, organized religion has had a direct role in establishing most marriages. But in too many cases the church has often acted as a **"blessing machine"** that has no more impact on the couple than a justice of the peace. Too many churches have deteriorated to being little more than a **"wedding factory"** offering a borrowed chapel, a hired pastor, and a rented organist.

IDEAS FOR BEING A MARRIAGE SAVER

Both premarital sexual activity and cohabitation should be denounced by Christians—just as Paul denounced it for the church at Corinth. (See 1 Cor. 6:13, 18-20; 10:13.)

Teachers, utilize the opportunities you have to teach others in small-group settings.

Pastors, preach on these issues, taking advantage of annual family emphases and sermon series.

Counselors, advise couples of the dangers and point them to the biblical truths.

Couples and *individuals,* encourage others you know to become acquainted with these truths and facts by sharing with them a copy of this book and God's Word.

Biblical References

Malachi 2:8, 13-16; 1 Corinthians 6:13, 18-20; 10:13; 1 Thessalonians 4:3; Hebrews 13:4

Other Resources

1. *Marriage Savers* by Michael McManus (Zondervan, 1993), chapters 2 and 3.
2. Have your pastor view *Marriage Savers Resource Collection,* especially video programs 1, 2, and 3.

A N S W E R   3

Insuring Marriage

Help Your Church Insure Future Marriages

Gallup Polls reveal that less than 20 percent of Americans who get married have had any premarital counseling. And those who got such counseling are *just as likely* to divorce as those who had no marriage preparation.

For many years the Catholic Church has recognized that the main reason most marriages fail is poor communication. Most U.S. Catholic dioceses take five steps to improve communication between the man and woman who want to be married. If you are engaged, consider these steps for you and your future mate. If you are married or if you are a church leader, you can use these steps and develop an engagement preparation process for couples you know.

1. Participate in a premarital inventory. An inventory is given to help the couple objectively assess the strengths and weaknesses of their relationship. The usual format is a list of questions that force the couple to really think about areas of their lives that will later become issues of potential conflict. More detail will follow in Answer 9.

Because they're in love and agree about one or

two important areas—such as religion or how many children they plan to have—couples feel that everything else will work out.

In reality, a marital inventory pulls no punches. It says without flinching if there are areas of incompatibility or issues of conflict. These issues must be resolved *before* the marriage or they will become the ammunition for the "war" to follow.

The Catholic tradition of a pre-Cana preparation for the engaged couple is a good model. Couples who are given adequate premarital counsel and work with an inventory are much more likely to avoid later conflicts.

My wife, Harriet, and I work with engaged couples in our church. We are always amazed to see how the inventory points up such differences. Many are cultural; some are religious. I recall one quiet young Asian girl who was engaged to a boisterous Italian. Whenever she went to visit his family, she felt terrible confusion and conflict because the family members were so loud and opinionated. She thought they were angry. Her background was different. When they visited her family, everyone was so subdued and quiet that her fiance felt uneasy.

The inventory also helps point out the differences in family leadership styles. Dave and Cathy came from two distinctly different homes. Dave's mom took more of a leadership role, and Dave was like his mom. Cathy, on the other hand, was more submissive. Her family tended to be individualistic, with no one person "in charge." Harriet and I told them that each needed to work on these areas. If not, their relationship would become one-sided, with Dave "taking charge" and making most of the decisions unilaterally.

In areas of communication, Dave and Cathy learned that each had different styles of sharing. Cathy liked to talk things out, discuss and review, consider and talk some more. Dave, on the other hand, said little. And when the issue was a "touchy" one, he'd clam up completely, so conflicts were never resolved.

The couple learned from the inventory that there were *many* issues on which they disagreed. They decided to work on these issues so that they could have a loving marriage relationship.

In every instance of our premarital counseling, we have been told by the couples that they were grateful for having taken the inventory. We know from personal experience that it saves marriages.

2. Establish a relationship with a mentor couple. Solidly married couples should mentor younger ones. The Catholic Church recruits couples to assist the parish priest in the premarital instruction of younger couples. The mentor couples are often called "coordinating couples," and they review an inventory with the engaged couple. The mentor couple also makes suggestions on how the engaged couple might handle the conflicts or misunderstandings the inventory brings to light.

Harriet and I have mentored fifteen young couples over the past three years. It has been and continues to be a rewarding experience. We know we have been "marriage savers" with many young couples.

We have also trained 22 mentor couples at our church who are now uniquely qualified to help engaged couples. Why? Their greatest credential is that they have marriages which have lasted an average of 30 years!

Every church has couples with solid marriages who could pass on their wisdom to younger ones. The young engaged couples benefit greatly from the experience—successes and failures—of the mature married mentor couples.

Mentor couples are the single greatest resource churches have to save troubled marriages. Yet few older couples are ever invited to become mentors. Churches are missing out by not tapping into this unique and valuable resource.

3. Attend a weekend retreat for engaged couples. One proven retreat is Engaged Encounter. Nearly 35,000 couples attend annually.

Married couples share intimate stories with engaged couples. Then 20-25 engaged couples go into a quiet personal retreat to write reflections and share them privately with their intended spouse. The sharing is on tough questions like.

"What things do I talk to others about more easily than with you?"

"What doubts do I have in marrying you?" "What things about you make me angry?"

So intensive is Engaged Encounter that a tenth of the engagements break. Good! Better the broken engagement than the broken marriage later with two kids. More information on Engaged Encounter is included in Answer 11.

Not every church can utilize Engaged Encounter. Your church can plan an effective weekend for engaged couples using *Counsel for the Nearly and Newly Married* or *I Take Thee to be My Spouse.*

4. Participate in lectures, writing, and dialogue related to premarital issues.

Lectures and workshops can focus on such issues as how the couple will handle their money, communication, and conflict resolution. Other classes and workshops can deal with other problems newly married couples are likely to encounter.

Writing and dialogue is essential. Couples fill out workbooks sparking thought on issues that are easily ignored in the glow of romance. Often the dialogue is with other engaged couples and older, solidly married ones.

5. Spend time preparing for marriage.
Catholics typically require six months of marriage preparation from the time the couple first meets with clergy until the wedding date. In communities where religious leaders from various churches have adopted a Community Marriage Policy (see Answer 25), four-month minimum preparation is required.

The previous four steps will require time to complete. You may find that you will need more than four or six months.

Sadly, most churches have no minimum time requirement, no mentor couples, no required writing or dialogue, no retreats, no premarital inventory, and no lectures on substantive issues.

These are the elements that work! Research bears out the fact that each of these factors makes a remarkable contribution to the success of new marriages. Collectively, they will help you and your church be a marriage saver.

Biblical References
Job 12:12-13; Psalm 32:8; Isaiah 28:26; 42:16; Titus 2:1-5

Other Resources
1. *Marriage Savers* by Michael McManus (Zondervan, 1993), chapters 2-7.

2. *Marriage Savers Resource Collection,* video programs 2 and 3.

3. *Counsel for the Nearly and Newly Married* by Ernest White and James E. White (Convention Press, 1992).

4. *I Take Thee to Be My Spouse* compiled by David Apple (Convention Press, 1992).

Insuring Marriage

Help Teenagers Abstain from Sex

Teenagers who remain chaste until they marry **reduce their odds of divorce.** Only 14 percent of virgin brides in 1980-83 were divorced by 1988; 24 percent of non-virgins had divorced. Today, less than 10 percent are virgins when they marry.

Four proven programs teach abstinence, challenge teenagers to remain sexually pure, and prepare them for marriage. True Love Waits and Why Wait? are church-based. Sex Respect and Postponing Sexual Involvement are school-based.

TRUE LOVE WAITS

The Southern Baptist Convention has pioneered a major answer to the question of teen chastity by co-ordinating a national campaign called True Love Waits. Between April, 1993 and July, 1994, hundreds of thousands of teenagers signed a covenant card stating:

> *Believing that true love waits, I make a commitment to God, myself, my family, those I date, my future mate, and my future children to remain sexually pure until the day I enter a covenant marriage relationship.*

When asked why he signed a card, Julio Hernandez, 17, said, "I just want to save myself for my future wife. I think the only gift I can give her is myself. One key reason is that I want to remain close to God. It keeps my mind free."

True Love Waits did not end with the campaign. It is now an annual emphasis promoted in churches and communities each February. You can provide True Love Waits for new youth as encouragement to teenagers who have made the commitment.

Why Wait?

Josh McDowell has spoken to more than eight million college students. One of his frequent themes is the need for chastity. He became suspicious about what churches were teaching youth about sex and conducted a Teen Sex Survey. It revealed that 75 percent of church youth in even the most conservative denominations *learned little or nothing about sex from their church.* And the study revealed that 43 percent of church youth aged 18 have had intercourse, *only slightly less than unchurched youth.*[1]

McDowell created four videos (15 minutes each) called "NO! The Positive Answer" you can use with your church youth. He tells teenagers, "God has given you rules to protect and provide for you." The video series uses humor, music, role playing, and the kids themselves speak out on the pressures, fears, and victories in the sexual arena.

Sex Respect

A former high school teacher, Coleen Kelly Mast, has developed an abstinence-based course now offered in several thousand high schools. In addition to the student text there is a Parent's Guide to help parents discuss this tough issue with a teen. **Parents need the help.** Only 8 percent of fathers and 15 percent of mothers have ever talked with their teen about sex.[2]

Sex Respect teaches students how to handle the "lines" they'll hear:

"You would, if you loved me!"

"If you loved me, you wouldn't ask!"

Mrs. Mast believes most sex education is "too narrow, focused only on the physical, saying if you get rid of the physical consequences of premarital sex (via contraceptives or abortion), all will be OK. That's a lie. There are serious emotional and physical effects. Even adults have difficulty getting over a sexual relationship. Teens are being taught they can act on any impulse and not have to face the consequences. How can we create a healthy society when its citizens have not learned self-control?"

The Institute for Research and Evaluation in Salt Lake City studied the long-term impact of the course and concluded: "After two years, those taking Sex Respect had pregnancy rates that were *half* of those students not in the program, but attending the same schools."

POSTPONING SEXUAL INVOLVEMENT

Postponing Sexual Involvement (PSI) is an excellent course for eighth graders in public schools.

In the 1970s, Dr. Marion Howard created a sex education program like that often found in most public schools—five classes of discussions on human sexuality, human decision-making, family planning, and contraceptives. It flopped.

Dr. Howard concluded: "Simply providing young teenagers with such information was not effective in changing sexual behavior." She also decided that the best way to reach young teens is through role models using slightly older teenagers.

These teens give information, identify pressures, and discuss problem situations. The teenage leaders produce greater and more lasting effects than adults, says Dr. Howard.

A key focus of her course is helping teenagers

learn how to say "no" without hurting the others. Its premise is that young people are often pressured into doing things they really do not want to do.

To measure PSI's impact, research indicated that after a year "students who had not had PSI were as much as **five times** more likely to have initiated sex than were those who had taken it: 20 percent vs. 4 percent!" Also, the number of teen pregnancies fell by a third over a five-year period!

Biblical References
1 Corinthians 6:13-20; 10:13; 1 Thessalonians 4:3; Titus 2:11-12

Other Resources
1. **True Love Waits**, 127 Ninth Avenue North, Nashville, TN 37234. Planning kit available.

2. **Why Wait?** P.O. Box 1330, Wheaton, IL 60189 1-800-222-JOSH

3. **Sex Respect**, P.O. Box 349-M, Bradley, IL 60915.

4. **Postponing Sexual Involvement**, Box 26158, Grady Memorial Hospital, 80 Butler St. S.E., Atlanta, GA 30335.

5. *Christian Sex Education Series,* (LifeWay Press, 1993, Call 1-800-458-2772.) *Sex! What's That?* (for preadolescents) by Susan Lanford; *Sexuality: God's Gift* (for adolescents) by Ann Cannon; *Christian Sex Education: Parents and Church Leaders Guide* compiled by Jimmy Hester.

6. *Marriage Savers Resource Collection,* video program 2.

7. *Marriage Savers* by Michael McManus (Zondervan, 1993), chapter 4.

---

[1]Josh McDowell and Dick Day, *Why Wait?* (San Bernardino: Here's Life Publishers, Inc., 1987), 99.

[2]E. S. Roberts, D. Kline, and J. Cagon: *Family Life and Sexual Learning of Children, Vol 1* (Cambridge: Population Education, Inc., 1981), 32.

A N S W E R 5

Insuring Marriage

Beware of Sexual Entrapments

What's wrong with sex for those in their 20s and 30s who are in love? Conventional wisdom says this is not only harmless but beneficial. However, emotional intimacy with someone other than your spouse or future spouse can lead to unfaithfulness and a lack of trust in marriage.

Harriet and I have worked as mentors to about 15 couples in recent years. "Jerry" and "Pam" had dated for four years in their early twenties, broke off for two years, and recently dated again.

We administered PREPARE, a premarital inventory in which they individually responded to 125 statements.

They scored 90 percent on their "Sexual Relationship," but 0 percent on "Religious Orientation." She was a Christian—he wasn't. They knew of that difference and were somewhat concerned about it.

However, I was puzzled by other answers. On the statement, "We have discussed the responsibilities of a father in raising children," Jerry marked "Agree." Pam marked "Disagree." I asked him to explain his answer. He said. "We *have* discussed the role of a father in raising children."

Pam broke in, "We have *not* discussed it to the

point of making a decision."

Jerry replied, "We've discussed things like who'll watch the children. She says she wants to stay home and not work. I feel that to survive, we have to have two incomes. We'll have to put the kids in day care. If you live in northern Virginia, it will be too expensive without two incomes."

Pam was dumbfounded—on two levels. First, this was hardly a *discussion* of the role of the father in bringing up children. It was more of a *declaration* by Jerry. Secondly, she was hearing— much more clearly than ever before—Jerry's absolute denial of her being a stay-at-home mom.

Trying to mediate, I said, "You don't have to live in northern Virginia to do your kind of work. You could live in Lynchburg."

"Lynchburg?" he asked.

"In Lynchburg, you could buy a home for $60,000, and Pam could be a stay-at-home mom," I explained. It was a point of view he did not want to consider.

"It's unrealistic. I work at three jobs now. I can't imagine making a mortgage payment with one income."

Pam's brow furrowed. She was hearing something from him on this issue that she had not heard before. Finally, Harriet got suspicious, and asked, "Jerry, do you really want to have children?"

He leaned back, looked down and said, "No— not particularly."

My eyes darted over to Pam. Her mouth dropped in shock and horror. She'd never heard that he did not want to be a father before. But why not? They'd gone together for nearly *five years*—how could they not talk about it?

The answer is that they were 90 percent compatible on sexual issues. Pam, although a Christian, had given in to the pressure and became sexually active with Jerry. And it became a trap.

Instead of talking through key issues about their relationship, sex gave them the illusion of intimacy. Yet it prevented them from really understanding each other.

Pam was wasting her time with such a person. He was hostile to her faith and wouldn't go to church with her. As is true in so many cases, Pam made the mistake of thinking she could change Jerry. Instead of spending nearly five years with Jerry, she would have been better off going to a church with a strong singles group where she might have met a Christian man who shared her values.

Sex before marriage is a trap that fools one (or both) of the partners into thinking they have a closeness and intimacy that will make the relationship work. But it's merely a facade. **Intimacy is more than a sexual relationship. Chastity before marriage is a proven way to avoid divorce**.

If you find yourself in this entrapment, seek counsel from your pastor, a counselor, a mentor couple, or a Christian friend. If you recognize a dating couple that may be in this entrapment, share your concern. Chastity before marriage is a proven way to avoid divorce.

Biblical References
1 Corinthians 6:13-20; 1 Thessalonians 4:3; Hebrews 4:15,.16; James 1:12

Other Resources
1. *Marriage Savers* by Michael McManus (Zondervan, 1993), chapter 5.
2. *Marriage Savers Resource Collection:* "Helping Singles and Seriously Dating Couples."

A N S W E R 6

Insuring Marriage

Don't Live Together in a Trial Marriage

Fearing a divorce, millions of seriously dating couples have begun "trial marriages" in which they live together but are not married. Cohabitation is particularly common among children of divorce.

In March 1970, the Census Bureau reported that 523,000 unmarried couples were living together. By 1993 the number soared to 3.5 million couples.

How many marriages are preceded by a period where the couples simply live together? The University of Wisconsin's *National Survey of Families and Households* estimates that only 8 percent of first marriages were preceded by cohabitation in the late 1960s, but more than half were preceded by cohabitation by 1990.

In remarriage (where one or both parties have been divorced), **two-thirds** lived together first.

The *National Survey of Families and Households* reports that cohabiting couples face two facts:

1. At least one person in 90 percent of the couples wants to marry, but 40 percent of the couples who live together *break up before marriage* after about 1.3 years.

Many then suffer from "premarital divorce." Still, they are likely to try living with Partner B, then C, and end up at age 37 wondering why they're not married.

The result: never-married Americans have **doubled** from 21 million people in 1970 to 42 million by 1992.

2. Marriages that are preceded by living together have 50 percent higher disruption rates (divorce or separation) than marriages without premarital cohabitation according to the *National Survey of Families and Households*. The normal divorce rate is about 50 percent. Thus, those who live in a "trial marriage" first face a 75 percent divorce rate after 10 years![1]

Marriage is not a shoe one can try on before buying it!

But for millions, for whom *cohabitation has become a substitute for a covenant marriage*, they've encountered a disease that kills the marriage at the front end of the relationship. And it's a disease that spreads to affect matrimony for those who marry *after* living together.

The answer is plain: **Do not cohabit!** If you are living with someone, consider the odds. If you know of a couple living in a trial marriage, share with them the odds. Of 100 couples who begin a trial marriage, 40 don't marry. Of 60 couples who do wed, there are 45 divorces after 10 years. That's an *85 percent failure rate*.

With a mere 15 percent chance of success, why do young people, especially Christian couples, consider relationships that disregard Scripture? Paul was succinct: "Flee from sexual immorality" (1 Cor. 6:18). Hebrews 13:4 is also clear: "Marriage should be honored by all and the marriage bed be kept pure, for God will judge the adulterer and all the sexually immoral."

Fortunately, there is a better way for seriously dating couples to structure their relationship. Instead of an 85 percent failure rate after they marry, as with cohabitation, God's plan gives *a 90 percent chance of success*!

Biblical References
Romans 6:1-2, 14; 1 Corinthians 6:13-20; 2 Corinthians 5:17; Galatians 5:16,17; Hebrews 13:4

Other Resources
1. *Marriage Savers* by Michael McManus (Zondervan, 1993), chapters 2 and 5.
2. *Marriage Savers Resource Collection,* video program 2.

---

[1]Larry Bumpass, *National Survey of Families and Households* Working Papers #2 and #5, Center for Demography and Ecology at the University of Wisconsin, 1989.

A N S W E R   7

Insuring Marriage

Seriously Dating Couples Can Avoid Mistakes

If cohabitation is the worst step that seriously dating couples can take, what is the best step? Consider Relationship Instruction, developed by Dr. Jim A. Talley, a former pastor and presently a marital therapist who has worked with over 13,000 single adults over a 24 year period. Relationship Instruction is the best way for couples who are not yet engaged to be sure they've chosen the right mate.

Look at the results. Since 1976, thousands of couples have signed the Relationship Instruction contract. Talley reports that fewer than 10 percent gave up and did not complete it. And, of all the seriously dating couples who did complete it, half of them did not marry. But of those who did marry, *less than 10 percent* have ended in divorce or separation. Relationship Instruction is "marriage insurance."

The demands of Relationship Instruction may seem unusual—even intimidating. The couple signs a contract—called the "Pre-requisites"—agreeing to specific, serious steps to promote spiritual maturity in Christ; build trust; develop agape love; and learn to control physical, emotional, and mental habits.

Requirements include:
- Read *Too Close Too Soon*
- Complete weekly workbook assignments.
- Complete an eight-session, four-month course (even if the relationship breaks up).
- Do not discuss an engagement.
- Do not date anyone else.
- Limit time together.
- Avoid sexual activity (to the point of calling the instructor or mentor couple if they exceed French kissing.)

The following is one area of a couple's relationship that is considered. The control of sexual activity is important in evaluating a relationship. If you are in a seriously dating relationship, complete this exercise.

HOW FAR?

If you are in a seriously dating relationship, circle the number that represents the highest level of physical involvement between you and your friend in the last 30 days.

1 Look
2 Touch
3 Lightly holding hands
4 Constantly holding hands
5 Light kiss
6 Strong kiss
7 French kiss
8 Fondling breasts
9 Fondling sexual organs
10 Sexual intercourse

If you circled number seven or higher, seriously consider where your physical involvement is taking you in your relationship.

Harriet and I have used Relationship Instruction over the years. We received a call one Saturday. "We went further than we should have last night," said Dave. "We're disappointed in ourselves, but we feel better about calling you. It's good that our church holds us accountable."

How do couples generally react to Relationship Instruction? "First, we have needed someone to be accountable to," said Cathy. "Second, the workbook gave us something concrete to do. For Dave to read my thoughts on paper meant that I had to be vulnerable."

Dave commented, "When you see it written down on paper, it seems more serious." He discovered by writing out his goals that he'd like to have his own business in five years. So he decided to do some free-lance work on Saturdays, to see if he could find the clients he'd need in order to go on his own.

Cathy added, "I feel sorry for the couples who don't go through this kind of preparation before marriage."

Another couple, Gary and Janine agreed. "Relationship Instruction helped us pace the relationship," says Gary. "Sexual discipline made my commitment more real to my partner. By (our) abstaining, she learned to trust me more."

Janine added, "It gave me a way to understand the person I was romantically inclined toward. I got a more objective picture of his likes, dislikes, what goals we have in common, what our financial situation was, our future as far as children."

Andrea, a divorcee who married twice-divorced Bob, said "It helped us put on the brakes. People who've been married before can easily jump the hurdles of the heart stuff and head into the physical part."

Bob adds "I had serious doubts . . . after two failures, I needed help to prepare for marriage."

These couples discovered that Relationship Instruction was a wonderful investment in building their relationship.

Biblical References
Deuteronomy 4:29; 29:9; Hosea 10:12; Philippians 4:9; Hebrews 11:6; James 1:5, 6

Other Resources
1. For information and to order Relationship Instruction workbooks and *Too Close Too Soon,* call 1-800-645-3761.

2. *Marriage Savers Resource Collection,* video program 2.

3. *Marriage Savers* by Michael McManus (Zondervan, 1993), chapters 5 and 6.

A N S W E R   8

Insuring Marriage

Learn from a Relationship That Doesn't Lead to Marriage

What if, despite your investment in Relationship Instruction, you learn there are still too many areas of incompatibility and your relationship falls apart? What happens if this process does not lead to marriage? Is there still a value in taking the course? Yes!

Half those taking Relationship Instruction do not marry—but **learn about themselves** and **how to build a future relationship.**

Consider "Liz" and "Sam," another couple we mentored, both of whom were in their 40s but had never married.

Sam explained his approach to women in nautical terms: "I love to take a woman out in my boat for a sail. Inevitably a little squall kicks up—an argument—and I think, 'She must not be God's person for me.' So I take her 'back to the dock.' But I finally realized I've been taking women back to the dock for 20 years. It's time I learned how to sail with one out of the harbor. And Relationship Instruction seems like a perfect way to do it."

The contractual nature of the course gave Liz a great sense of hope and freedom. For a year she'd been afraid of intimacy. "In our relationship," she said, "it was a monologue by him. He talked and I listened. It never became a dialogue until we started this process. Only then did I feel free to express myself."

And boy, did she ever! When Sam got to work on Monday he checked his "phone mail." There was Liz, with a 30 minute monologue on their relationship. "I was still afraid to say what I was feeling to him face to face, but I could do it on voice mail because I wasn't worried that he'd leave."

That happened several times, and Sam did feel like putting her "back on the dock," but he'd made the four-month commitment, and he honored it.

That summer Liz felt like getting out of the relationship, but she didn't. Later, it was Sam's turn to say he wanted out.

Harriet and I advised both of them to stop seeing each other for a few months. "You may find that there is a hole in your life that only she can fill," I told Sam. "But give her, and yourself, some space and time." They both agreed.

In the final session, we asked them "**What was the value of the course?**"

"First, it is a way of learning about yourself. Relationship Instruction gives a focus, and it definitely develops some communication skills," Liz told me. "Also, we were not really friends before, per se. If we had married, it would have been difficult. There was no foundation. Relationship Instruction showed us how to develop a relationship. Out of that we are becoming good friends, which is necessary in marriage"

Curiously, Sam came to similar conclusions. "I took the course because we wanted to learn about ourselves. This was the deepest sharing I have ever had with another person in my life. That's both the greatest and the scariest thing."

While the relationship did not work out, both of them grew. They learned they could build a deep relationship with another person—an important first for each of them. They emerged with not just a high respect for each other—but a much higher self-respect. By keeping the sexual element sharply limited, they can in clear conscience walk away from the relationship, feeling good about themselves and the other person.

Ten Steps in Working Through a Broken Relationship

Step 1   Deal with your emotions.

Step 2   Forgive yourself.

Step 3   Forgive the other person.

Step 4   Do not date for three to six months minimum to allow your emotions time to heal.

Step 5   Be cautious about entering into a long-term commitment with someone else.

Step 6   Get involved helping others.

Step 7   Treat yourself to something special.

Step 8   If negative emotions continue, seek help from a counselor or your pastor.

Step 9   Build same-sex friendships.

Step 10   Participate regularly in church and community activities.

Biblical References

Psalm 138:8; Proverbs 3:4-6; Isaiah 28:26; Philippians 1:9; 1 Thessalonians 4:1; 2 Timothy 1:7; 3:14-16

Other Resources

1. *Marriage Savers Resource Collection,* video program 2.

2. *Marriage Savers* by Michael McManus (Zondervan, 1993), chapters 5 and 6.

A N S W E R 9

Insuring Marriage

Use a Premarital Inventory to Identify Strengths and Weaknesses

Dr. James Dobson in *Love for a Lifetime* writes: "A dating relationship is designed to conceal information, not reveal it. Each partner puts his or her best foot forward, hiding embarrassing facts, habits, flaws, and temperaments."[1]

Fortunately, there are ways to cut through those facades. A premarital inventory has the ability to predict marital success or failure *in time to do something about it*.

One of the best inventories is called PREPARE. It consists of 125 questions, asked of the man and woman separately. Their answers are compared by computer and returned to a qualified interpreter.

The man and woman indicate whether they agree or disagree with statements like:

> *I believe that most disagreements we currently have will decrease after marriage.*
> *I am concerned about my partner's drinking and/or smoking.*
> *I can easily share my positive and negative feelings with my partner.*

I wish my partner were more careful in spending money.

Each person is asked about the other person. What surfaces is a virtual X-ray of the relationship. Ten questions are asked in each of a dozen areas (finances, conflict resolution, sex, and differences in family background). The results tell if the couple agrees or disagrees on each question.

The inventory then gives the couple an objective and realistic assessment of their relative "Relationship Strengths" or "Growth Areas."

Harriet and I administered PREPARE to Dave, a journalist, and Cathy, an attractive nurse. They had known each other for nearly two years. Cathy was surprised that a simple questionnaire could probe the unexplored areas of their relationship.

In the evaluation, counselors focus first on the couple's "relationship strengths." So, we congratulated Cathy and Dave for their 90 percent agreement on religious orientation. But I noted that on "conflict resolution" they only scored 30 percent.

PREPARE goes beyond merely pointing out problems. Counselors are urged to help the couple find their own solutions by focusing on an issue and leading the couple through steps to resolve conflict. Learning how to resolve their conflicts is as important as the objective assessment of discovering what their areas of conflict are.

Successful marriages are built on good communication and conflict resolution skills. And the good news is these skills can be taught.

I tested that thesis by asking Dave and Cathy to define their current problem of conflict resolution.

Cathy said there were times she "gets the silent treatment" when she brings up a problem. Or Dave will say something "is fine" when he's really putting her off.

Dave replied, "I need time to think. Sometimes I

am not sure what to say. She has about 1,000 words on a subject, while I have about 50. She wears me out."

I asked, "How do you each contribute to the problem?"

Cathy said, "When he clams up on me, I put my answering machine on and don't take his call, even if I am home."

"So you give *him* the silent treatment!" I commented. She smiled.

Harriet and I asked for solutions tried in the past that were not successful. Next, we asked them to list all the possible solutions. They discussed these and other ideas, agreed on a combination of them, then decided what each should do to work toward a solution.

"That was a wall in our relationship," said Dave later, "and you gave us a stepladder over that wall."

Of 100,000 couples who take PREPARE annually, some 10,000 couples—a tenth—find so many problems, they actually decide to break their engagements.

But better a broken engagement than a broken marriage.

Those who do break their engagements invariably have such bad scores that they'd have probably divorced if they had gotten married.

A premarital inventory like PREPARE actually *helps couples avoid a bad marriage before it even begins!*

We were mentors of one couple who appeared to be "in love." But their scores ranged from 0 to only 30 percent. When we called them up to say we were ready to give them their results, the young woman told us, "We broke our engagement after we discussed PREPARE. I was nervous about the relationship, but this convinced me it would not work."

"You did the right thing," I replied.

There is another value of PREPARE. It provides a way for a mentor couple to relate to a couple and give them suggestions on how they might solve some of their conflicts.

Harriet and I are not professionals in marriage counseling, but in 29 years of marriage, we've learned to deal with conflict and other problems that threaten a relationship.

If you are getting married soon, or know a couple who is, and you do not know anyone who is trained to administer an inventory, contact the people at PREPARE/ENRICH. There are 25,000 pastors and counselors trained to administer the inventory. Ask for the name of someone in your area who is trained to offer the one-day seminar.

Biblical References

Deuteronomy 7:12; Job 36:11; Psalm 25:9; 37:4; James 1:5

Other Resources

1. **PREPARE/ENRICH**, Box 190, Minneapolis, MN 55440.

2. *Marriage Savers* by Michael McManus (Zondervan, 1993), chapter 6.

3. *Marriage Savers Resource Collection,* videos programs 2 and 3.

---

[1]James C. Dobson, *Love for a Lifetime* (Portland: Multnomah, 1987), 22.

A N S W E R 1 0

Insuring Marriage

Help Insure and Save Marriages by Being a Mentor Couple

The greatest untapped resource to insure and save marriages are **married couples who can act as mentors for younger couples.** If you have been married 20-50 years, you have much to offer. You've learned the secrets of successful marriage. As a result, you hold a great store of wisdom and experience.

These couples know how to communicate, resolve conflict, and cherish one another. Young couples would love to tap their wisdom.

Solidly married couples are a treasure that can be found in the pews of any church. Yet very few churches have considered inviting them to mentor engaged or seriously dating couples.

Catholic churches are the exception. For 15-plus years, older couples have been mentoring engaged couples. These mentors, or "coordinating couples," work in one of three ways, beginning with the most useful and intensive interventions.

1. Engaged Encounter. Mentor couples donate a weekend of time to lead a group of engaged couples in an intensive retreat. This is by far the best experience for the engaged couples, but also the most demanding for the married couples in terms of energy and time.

2. Evenings For the Engaged. Typically, mentor couples give three evenings of time to ask probing questions. They also share their own experience with the engaged couple.

One mentor explained: "One after another is shocked by what their fiancés are saying: 'What do you mean, we will spend Christmas at *your* folks' house? Who says *you* will manage the checkbook?' Clearly, tough issues had not been faced by many couples until they were asked probing questions. By the third evening, all the couples love the experience because they are learning so much. After the weddings, many keep in contact with us. They feel they have someone they can turn to if they get in trouble. It has been a very satisfying experience."

3. Pre-Cana Workshops. Pre-Cana Workshops are three all-day Saturday sessions. Engaged couples must write in workbooks, read each other's comments and talk about them with each other— perhaps with a table of three other engaged couples led by a mentor couple.

Our Mentoring Model

Harriet and I have fashioned a different mentoring model at our church. We have trained 22 couples whose marriages have lasted an average of 30 years. They work with seriously dating and engaged couples on a one-to-one basis. Our mentors also meet with one couple privately in their home and administer the PREPARE inventory. When the computerized report is returned, the mentors go over the results with their assigned couple in two or three sessions in their home.

Mentor training includes having the mentor couple take an ENRICH inventory, which raises many of the same issues as PREPARE. This strengthens the mentor couple as well as trains them to work with engaged couples.

The Mentor's View

Mentors seem to find a new appreciation of Jesus' admonition, "Give and it will be given to you" (Luke 6:38).

Mentor Ted Kupelian said, "Of the 12 years I've served as a leader, we've enjoyed it as much as anything. The two of us working as a couple has made it the most rewarding work."

Bob Stenstrom, another mentor, said that PRE-PARE was "very helpful to our couple. The feedback was the gist of our two sessions together and a good springboard to a number of other issues. It supports sharing our own experiences without being pontifical or pious. It was invaluable in developing the insights into their burgeoning relationship."

Joe Ann Stenstrom, Bob's wife of 30-plus years, added, "In our experience of being a mentor couple, one of the best parts is getting to know your own relationship. It forces you to analyze what makes your husband-wife relationship work. In taking the (ENRICH) inventory, it confirmed some of our own areas of compatibility—and differences that keep life interesting. *It shows why you got married in the first place!"*

Reactions of the Engaged

"Very valuable experience," wrote one young groom-to-be in an evaluation. "PREPARE and mentoring are so good that all those planning to marry should be required by law to take this course!"

"The highlight of the course was the mentoring," said Roberto Anson. "Bob and Joe Ann Stenstrom were fantastic. I heard their wisdom and saw how they functioned as a team. Through them and PRE-PARE I learned a lot."

Hugh, another mentor, said, "The engaged see that we're open and willing to be vulnerable, and tell them about our private life. That, in turn, allows them to open up more of themselves."

Mentoring in Perspective

A pastor cannot usually do all the premarital counseling in his church. Also, it's valuable to have both a male and a female perspective. Harriet is always sensitive to emotional issues that escape me. And I pick up on male frustrations she doesn't see. I tend to pay attention to the *ideas* being expressed, but she picks up on the *feelings* and body language, every bit as important as verbal communication.

The apostle Paul said the job of the pastor is "to prepare God's people for works of service" (Eph. 4:12). What more important service is there than being a marriage saver?

Biblical References

Isaiah 30:21; Philippians 1:9; 3:14-16; 1 Thessalonians 4:1

Other Resources

1. *Marriage Savers* by Michael McManus (Zondervan, 1993), chapter 7.

2. *Marriage Savers Resource Collection,* video programs 2, 3, and 4.

A N S W E R 11

Participate in a Premarital Retreat to Improve Communication Skills

Since three-fifths of all divorces are the result of poor communication, the best step you can take before the wedding ceremony to improve your communication skills is to attend a weekend retreat for engaged couples. Your church can develop a weekend retreat using resources like *Counsel for the Nearly and Newly Married,* or *Communication and Intimacy: Covenant Marriage.* Or, invite an effective conference leader to train couples.

Or you can attend Engaged Encounter, an intensive weekend retreat developed by Catholics, and since adopted by mainline and evangelical Protestant churches. The aim of Engaged Encounter is "to reduce the number of potential divorces, strengthen family ties, and reaffirm the biblical notion of covenant."

Its motto is:

> **"A wedding is but a day, but a marriage is for a lifetime."**

Engaged Encounter begins with a presentation of views of what a Christian marriage ought to be. After the presentation, each engaged couple is asked to go off together and write answers to some questions, read each other's reflections, then discuss them in private. The couples are asked to answer some tough questions:

"What about you makes me angry?"

"What doubts do I have in marrying you?"

"What differences between us might cause a problem if not discussed now—temperaments, children, past relationships, etc.?"

Challenging questions! But necessary ones.

This pattern repeats itself on other topics such as "Openness and Communication" and "Signs of a Closed Relationship."

More questions and private talk follow.

"How do I feel about committing myself to loving you 100 percent for the rest of my life?"

"How is God working in our engagement?"

"How will we reflect God's love after our wedding?"

All of that is covered before lunch on Saturday! Later the engaged couples focus on the myriad of practical decisions in marriage: whether to have children, when, how many, and how to discipline them.

Another session focuses on "Sex and Sexuality." A biblical perspective on sex as a gift from God leads to a talk on how to be unselfish and giving.

In "Plan of Life," money issues are covered:

"Who pays the bills?"

"How much money will go into savings?"

"What is the desired role of prayer to your long-term goals?"

On Saturday night this intensity is relieved with an informal dialogue between all couples on some hot questions:

"Is premarital sex a sin?"

"How important is sex in marriage?"

"What if my mate is unfaithful?"

On Sunday morning the couples discuss

"Forgiveness in Marriage" or "How to Share Vulnerability."

The weekend closes with a joyous time of worship and communion.

Reactions?

"This weekend showed me I have a lot of fears, mistrust, and difficulties risking honesty first with myself and then with my fiancé. It made me realize that commitment and love are things I have never taken seriously before," said one participant.

"It was a painful, emotional, draining, tearful, joyful, releasing, and finally peaceful experience," said one woman.

What engaged couple would not want to have a focused weekend in preparing for marriage? Plan one for your church or find out how to attend an Engaged Encounter weekend near you.

Biblical References
Leviticus 25:17; Proverbs 15:33; Matthew 18:4; 23:12; Colossians 3:9-10, 12-15

Other Resources
1. For more information on Engaged Encounter:

Protestants: Call Dave and Sue Edwards (303) 753-9407.

Catholics: Call Dave and Millie Florijan (412) 487-5116.

2. *Marriage Savers* by Michael McManus (Zondervan, 1993), chapter 7.

3. *Marriage Savers Resource Collection,* video program 3.

Insuring Marriage

Invest Time and Energy in Marriage Preparation

Engaged couples should seek out the most rigorous marriage preparation to insure having the same mate for life.

Recently Harriet and I went to a friend's wedding. The service and reception were wonderful. Don was as handsome as the bride was beautiful.

But nine days before the wedding Don called to ask about PREPARE. I explained how useful the inventory was, and how we use it to mentor young couples. Don asked, "How long does it take to get the results?"

"About 10 days," I replied. "They're sent to Minneapolis for computer scoring, then they're returned."

He then asked, "Can you hand score the answers, rather than have it sent off?"

"No. Why do you ask?"

"Well, I'm getting married in just nine days, and feel shaky about it, to be honest." What a time to feel shaky! I'd talked to Don six weeks earlier, and urged him then to take PREPARE. I sent him my book, *Marriage Savers,* but he hadn't looked at it until now and he began to panic.

In reading about PREPARE, Don realized that he should have taken it as a way to be sure that he had chosen the right woman, as well as for an objective assessment of the strengths and weaknesses of their relationship.

"Twice my pastor encouraged me to postpone the wedding," Don confessed. That was a red flag. His pastor, who knew them both, felt they were rushing into marriage.

I told Don that they could either take PREPARE before the wedding, and have the results after the honeymoon, or when they got back they could take ENRICH, a similar inventory—for married couples—that measures marriage satisfaction and relational compatibility.

Needless to say, neither step would help a person like Don who wasn't sure about getting married in nine days. What if their scores were poor? A tenth of couples who take PREPARE break their engagements, thus avoiding a bad marriage before it begins.

The trouble is, as almost every pastor will testify, it's extremely difficult to convince couples who have set a wedding date to invest time and energy in marriage preparation. Maybe one (or both) of them is afraid such a step might threaten their wedding.

Therefore, it seems a bit idealistic to expect the couple to give this matter priority unless there is a standard.

Both churches and the state should demand a minimum time and a number of certain prescribed steps of marriage preparation before couples can marry.

Sound radical? Not at all. Remember that most Catholic dioceses require *six months* of marriage preparation, and communities adopting Community Marriage Policies are requiring a minimum of *four months*. That six months can be filled with premarital testing, work with a mentor couple, a weekend retreat, and classes and lectures. That time ensures reality to penetrate romance.

In America, engagements are most often looked at as merely a time to plan for a wedding and a honeymoon. This is naive.

Engagements are a proven time to test a relationship to see if it has the resiliency to last for a lifetime. Preparation should be rigorous.

If you are planning a wedding for yourself or involved with one for a family member or friend, it is important that time be taken for preparation.

Yet we know that marriage preparation is a weak link. Couples do not think seriously enough about this need. That is why we should help them by making such preparation *mandatory.*

Engaged couples need to search for the most rigorous marriage preparation programs. If it's not possible to find such a program in a church in your community, couples should seek out a demanding marriage preparation inventory and workbook.

Biblical References
Psalm 32:8; Isaiah 2:3; Proverbs 6:23; Hebrews 4:12; James 1:5, 21-25

Other Resources
1. *Marriage Savers* by Michael McManus (Zondervan, 1993), chapters 6 and 12.

2. *Marriage Savers Resource Collection,* video program 3.

3. *Counsel for the Nearly and Newly Married,* by Ernest White and James E. White (Convention Press, 1993).

4. *Before You Say "I Do": Study Manual,* by W. Roberts and N. Wright (Harvest House, 1978).

Newlyweds Can Learn to Resolve Conflict

After six months of marriage, half of all couples witness dramatic increases in the frequency of arguments. They're often surprised at how critical they have become of their mate. Doubts emerge. They wonder *if they really married the right person.*

Before the wedding, in the glow of romance, everyone's mate is "perfect." After the wedding, often on the honeymoon, disenchantment creeps in. One of the partners gets upset, put down, or has feelings hurt. Soon, one or both of the partners feel "trapped" by their marriage.

Eventually, though, couples can reach maturity. Things finally smooth out for them—or else they go on to separation and divorce!

How can couples, caught in the sudden horror of this disenchantment, be helped to discover this maturity? Harriet and I faced such a specific case.

Heather and Peter asked to sit in our class. They had been married three months. Heather had a quiet sadness about her that seemed unusual for a newlywed. Peter was aloof and impatient.

We suggested that they take ENRICH, the marital inventory similar to PREPARE. "The biggest thing I've encountered is a lack of communication,"

Heather told us. ENRICH turned out to be an X-ray of their relationship. In 6 of 13 areas surveyed, their scores were only 10 to 20 percent in agreement.

We began our interpretation of their scores by praising relationship strengths. "One area of real strength in your marriage is your agreement on basic religious questions. For example, since you both feel your faith is important to your relationship, you can use it to help you bridge problems. When you argue, stop and pray for wisdom.

"But in communication, Heather, you say you're afraid to tell your partner what you think or ask him for what you want. Yet Peter wishes you were more willing to share your feelings with him. Your score says you both have serious arguments over unimportant issues."

We discussed their communication techniques, then I observed an area of conflict. "Peter, you wish she was more thrifty. And you see a substance abuse issue. What do you mean by that?" Peter referred to Heather's smoking problem.

"That's not a problem," Heather snapped. "Sure . . . sometimes I have a cigarette, but not more than *once every two weeks.*"

I said, "Well, this seems to be an area of conflict. How do you resolve your conflicts?"

"We both get frustrated," Peter sighed. He looked at Heather, and barked, "And you *are* driven to smoke. "

They said many of their conflicts were over money, a typical area of dispute among newlyweds. Peter owned an old home but had let it run down. Heather was trying to fix it up. But Peter thought she was spending too much money and time on it. She was hurt because "all he does is criticize." She added, "You express your feelings but always get shot down, so you don't want to share again."

They asked how Harriet and I argued. I replied, "Our relationship is always more important than the issue in dispute, so we want to be in consensus on any decision, especially involving money."

Harriet added, "If we can't resolve an issue, we'll just postpone making a decision about it."

I asked them to describe their areas of conflict. Peter replied, "I go off to work and get beat up at work, but Heather doesn't have that aggravation. She doesn't have a job—which we agree on—but all of her friends from school are 'breeding' and she's got a book she wants to write—"

Heather interrupted. "Wait a minute! *I have been hugely busy.* I'm working on the other house, still have thank-you notes from the wedding to write." Then she paused. "But he's right about the book. What I have in mind is a Christian book." Heather's eyes began to sparkle as she shared her dream of writing. "My mother's closest friend has written 'conversations with Jesus' and I'd—"

Peter interrupted her this time. "That's just my point. I kill myself at work but lose respect for her when she uses all her time on errands and little things that don't matter, then doesn't work on the good things. I'm working hard to free her to do work that we both believe to be important and creative. I mean, she's good at writing—she shouldn't be doing all these petty little things."

Finally. Here was the source of his anger. But now his anger was controlled and as he spoke, Heather was hearing his point of view as for the first time. She watched him with affection as she witnessed his love and respect for her.

"He's never said that before," she said softly. "He's right. I really *do* want to write. It combines three loves of my life—things of God, words, and the things dear to me. But I guess I've been procrastinating . . ." It was a special moment. From that point I knew they'd be successful in working out their disputes.

Heather turned to Harriet and me. "I'm taking

Peter's words to me as God giving me encouragement and admonition, and I want you two to help me be accountable."

Heather smiled, "This has been a wonderful evening." Gently, we pushed them out the door at 1:00 a.m. Their three-year marriage is doing well.

There are proven answers! First, ENRICH "shined a light on our relationship," as Heather said.

But the inventory would be useless unless the issues surfaced with another couple. A mature married couple can take the time to explore in depth examples from real life. A newlywed couple can more readily identify with the mentor couple. There is the sense that this couple has faced similar struggles and came through them successfully.

Use ENRICH and become a mentor couple. Any church that trains mentor couples to use PREPARE with seriously dating couples is already training those mentors to use ENRICH.

You can even continue to mentor the same couples you helped prepare for marriage.

Biblical References
Psalm 51:6; Proverbs 6:23; Matthew 7:24-25; James 1:2-4; 5:16

Other Resources
1. *Marriage Savers* by Michael McManus (Zondervan, 1993), chapter 8.

2. *Marriage Savers Resource Collection*, video program 4.

3. *I Take Thee as My Spouse*, compiled by David Apple (Convention Press, 1992).

4. *Covenant Marriage: Partnership and Commitment* by Diana Garland and Betty Hassler (LifeWay Press, 1989).

5. *Communication and Intimacy: Covenant Marriage* by Gary Chapman and Betty Hassler, (LifeWay Press, 1992).

A N S W E R   14

Insuring Marriage

Husband, Love Your Wife; Wife, Love Your Husband

Scripture contains principles for building a lifelong marriage. Memorize and apply them in your marriage relationship.

My brother, Tim, asked me to read the famous passage on love from 1 Corinthians 13 at his wedding. Later, he gave me the opportunity to say a few words from my heart. "Our culture says that *love is a feeling.* But Scripture defines *love as a decision,* an act of the will. Are you naturally patient? I'm not. I'm impatient. By nature I am naturally self-seeking, and easily angered. To be anything different takes an act of will on my part, and the help of God," I said.

"So, if I am to love Harriet, I must deny my natural feelings, and *decide* to be patient, to seek her good before mine, to hold my temper with her. I fall short, but I do a much better job cultivating these virtues with her now than when we married 28 years ago.

"And I've learned that when I take Paul's advice to *show* love, my *feeling* of love increases."

Too many say, "I don't love her (or him) any more. The feeling isn't there any more." My answer is simple—then **do something to show love**, and your feeling of love will return. Especially for men, feelings follow actions.

WHAT DOES SCRIPTURE SAY ABOUT LOVE IN MARRIAGE?

• Ephesians 5:21: "Submit to one another out of reverence for Christ."
In God's eyes, **the man and the woman are of equal importance**. Too many men quote verse 22 "Wives, submit to your husbands."—out of context, forgetting what was said in verse 21, that submission should be mutual. **Neither partner is superior or inferior. However, the partners have different roles**.

• Ephesians 5:22: "Wives, submit to your husbands."
That doesn't mean that wives are supposed to be doormats and have no position of importance. Rather, submission is a conscious decision to act in a loving way to your partner.

Looking again at 1 Corinthians 13, we're reminded that **the expected behavior is love**. But the modern view is flawed, often self-serving—"If you do this for me, I'll love you." There are strings attached. Biblical love is unconditional.

• Ephesians 5:23: "For the husband is the head of the wife as Christ is head of the church."
"The husband does this by *leading, loving, and caring*" according to David Sunde, speaker at a Family Life Conference of Campus Crusade for Christ. He also said: "We are accountable to God for our wives and children."

Leading
In the area of sex, Sunde asked if husbands had ever taken the lead and asked their wives, "How is

your sex life?" 1 Corinthians 7:4 says, "The husband's body does not belong to him alone but also to his wife."

Sunde continued, "Leadership involves managing your home. Do you have spiritual goals for your family, beyond going to church on Sunday? Do you have goals for your wife's intellectual development? That is leadership—setting goals." Men can take the responsibility to lead family devotions and go with the family to church and Sunday School.

I recall on another occasion Rev. Rick Yoder saying he once had a distressed call from a mother about her disruptive five-year-old son who bullied others. He agreed to see her, but told her to leave the boy at home and bring the father.

Yoder turned to the father and asked, "Do you spend much time with your son?" He said, "My job is very demanding." Yoder replied, "You played football in college. Have you ever thrown a football to your son? Who disciplines him?"

His wife began to sob, "Honey, I can't carry this burden any longer. I need help. I need you to take responsibility." So Yoder gave him two assignments: "Your son needs to spend time with his dad. And you send a note to the teacher saying you'll hold the son accountable for poor behavior."

A navy captain once told me, "I've let my job run away with my time, 80 hours a week. My perspective on the priority of my family has changed. I am going to schedule time for Christ and my family."

Loving
Sunde recalled that one day his wife asked, "David, why do you love me?"

He thought, "I need to work on taxes. I don't need this now." But instead he said, "I love you because the Bible says, 'Husbands, love your wives.' " She was disappointed.

Often, no sacrifice is required to show love, only thoughtfulness. One winter, Sunde cut a rose and brought it to his wife, saying, "Here is the last rose of the season for you."

She glowed, "You really love me!"

Caring

Ephesians 5:28-29 says, "Husbands ought to love their wives as their own bodies. He who loves his wife loves himself. After all, no one ever hated his own body, but he feeds and cares for it, just as Christ does the church."

Sunde said he often asks husbands, "What are your wife's greatest concerns?"

Most men get embarrassed, and admit, "I don't know."

He replies, "Caring is expressed when *she knows she is your priority.* Your wife should be the number one priority on your schedule."

Husbands and Wives Are to Love Each Other

Both partners in a marriage can learn from this model. Men, as well as women, need to be more loving and kind, more forgiving of their partner. True forgiveness may mean the complete surrender of our "rights" in order to rebuild a relationship.

The marriage process of "two becoming one" (Gen. 2:24) does not happen easily or automatically. It takes work. And it has to involve *tolerance—* the art of seeing things from the other's point of view.

Jay Kesler, in his book, *Restoring a Loving Marriage,* says, "Love is behavior, and it is possible to restore love by acting in obedience to God. . . . Only those who commit to trying harder will survive."[1]

When there is **mutual love** and a concern for the well-being of the other partner, both husbands and wives will discover the marriage that God intended for them.

Biblical References

Matthew 10:39; Mark 9:35; 1 Corinthians 13; Ephesians 5:18-25; Colossians 3:17-19; Hebrews 12:1-4; 1 John 4:18-20

Other Resources

1. *Quiet Times for Couples* by H. Norman Wright (Harvest House Publishers, 1990).

2. *Heirs Together of Life,* by Charles and Norma Ellis (Banner of Truth Books, P.O. Box 621 Carlisle, PA 17013).

3. *Marriage Savers* by Michael McManus (Zondervan, 1993), chapter 7.

4. *Restoring a Loving Marriage,* by Jay Kesler with Joe Musser (David C. Cook, 1989).

5. *Husband and Wives: The Best of Friends* by Otis and Deigie Andrews (LifeWay Press, 1994).

---

[1] Jay Kesler, *Restoring a Loving Marriage* (Elgin: David C. Cook, 1989), 138.

A N S W E R   15

Insuring
Marriage

Take Into Account Male and Female Differences

Many male-female conflicts are based on profound gender differences. Understanding them is an answer.

Ed, from New Jersey, had been in a troubled marriage for 31 years and had gone through marriage and family counseling to no avail. He came across the book, *Men Are From Mars, Women are From Venus* by John Gray[1], and wrote me: "I learned more in the first two dozen pages than from all of the counseling over the past thirty years."

Gray says men and women differ in all areas. They think and communicate differently; they feel, respond, love, and need differently. Someone who did not know better might even think that men and women were from entirely different planets.

So what happens is that men and women end up with all kinds of relationship problems by not understanding these differences.

MEN: HOW TO UNDERSTAND WOMEN

Women talk about problems to *feel better*. They're not really looking for solutions. Men, on the other hand, assume that if a woman is describing problems, she *wants an answer*.

In a class for engaged couples, Harriet and I role-played a situation from Gray's book of a wife coming home exhausted after work.

> Harriet (home after an exhausting day): "There's so much to do; I've no time for myself."
>
> Mike: "You should quit that job—it's too hard."
>
> Harriet: "But I like my job. They just want me to change."
>
> Mike: "Don't listen to them. Just do what you can."
>
> Harriet: "I forgot to call my aunt today."
>
> Mike: "Don't worry. She'll understand."
>
> Harriet: "With what she's going through? She needs me."
>
> Mike: "You worry too much. That's why you're unhappy."
>
> Harriet: "I am not unhappy. Why can't you just *listen* to me?
>
> Mike: "I *am* listening."
>
> Harriet: "Oh, why do I even bother?"

Thus, my "solutions" only made things worse. Women don't offer solutions when someone else is talking. They listen patiently, with empathy. Not until I had been married ten years did I learn my wife only wanted me to listen. Now when Harriet comes home, it's like this:

> Harriet: "There's so much to do, I have no time for me."
>
> Mike: "Sounds like you had a bad day."
>
> Harriet: "They expect me to change everything overnight."
>
> Mike (After a pause): "Hmmm."
>
> Harriet: "I even forgot to call my aunt."
>
> Mike: "Oh, really?"
>
> Harriet: "She needs me so much right now. I feel so bad."

Mike (Gives her a hug): "You're such a loving person!"

Harriet: "I love talking with you. You make me feel good."

Women also "score" gifts differently than men do. Each gift to her has equal value. A poem means as much as a new dress. So, men—here's some advice. **Devote more time to little things.** In returning home, give her a hug. Then ask specific questions about her day. Give her 20 minutes of your undivided attention—turn off the TV, wait to read the mail, and don't pick up the newspaper. Praise her looks. Surprise her with a love note.

WOMEN: HOW TO UNDERSTAND MEN

When your husband boasts to you about completing a big project, which he thinks is a big deal, don't treat it lightly.

If you want something, be direct and brief: "Would you please take out the trash?" He will respond. If he makes a mistake, don't say, "I told you so."

Another book on gender differences is *You Just Don't Understand* by Deborah Tannen. She says that boys and girls grow up in different cultures.

Boys play outside, in large groups that are hierarchically structured. Their groups have a leader who tells others what to do and resists what others propose. . . . Boys say, "Gimme that!" and "Get outta here!"

Girls play in small groups or in pairs; the center of a girl's life is a best friend. . . . In their games, such as jump rope or hopscotch, everyone gets a turn. Many of their activities (such as playing house) do not have winners and losers. They say, "Let's do this," and "How about doing that?" Girls are not accustomed to jockeying for status in an obvious way; they are more concerned that they be liked.[2]

If a man and woman are driving and she says, "Would you like to stop for a Coke?" he's likely to think about it, decide he'd rather get to their destination instead of stopping. So he'll answer honestly and say, "No."

But his wife's feelings will be hurt. He didn't realize she was not asking a simple factual question. Rather, she was opening negotiations on what they'll do next. But it went right over his head.

In short, **men and women are different**. Understanding differences can help us as marriage savers, both with our own marriages as well as when we guide others.

Biblical References
Genesis 1:27; Matthew 19:6; Galatians 5:25-26; Philippians 2:3

Other Resources
1. *Men Are From Mars, Women Are From Venus* by John Gray (HarperCollins, 1992).

2. *You Just Don't Understand* by Deborah Tannen (Ballantine Books, 1990).

---

[1]John Gray, *Men Are from Mars, Women Are from Venus* (New York: HarperCollins, 1992), 5-19.

[2]Deborah Tannen, *You Just Don't Understand* (New York: Ballantine Books, 1990), 43-44.

A N S W E R 16

Insuring Marriage

Make the Lord a Third Partner in Your Marriage

A study of 600 couples with long and successful marriages reveals their secret: **a Christ-centered home.**

That study by Dr. James Dobson was amplified in his book, *Love for a Lifetime.* He reported that a couple who prays together and depends on the Bible "for solutions to the stresses of living has a distinct advantage over the family with no faith. . . . Marriage and parenthood were **His** ideas, and He tells us in His Word how to live together in peace and harmony. Everything from handling money to sexual attitudes is discussed in Scripture."[1]

The purpose of marriage is not simply to draw two people together to carry on the human race. Rather, it's designed for us to more fully realize our natures. As two people become one in love and intimacy, their purpose is to also draw closer to God.

In marriage, two people execute a covenant to love and care for one another in mutual trust and faithfulness. You promise to love, honor, and care for each other in all circumstances so long as you both shall live. This is the kind of relationship God wants with us no matter what our marital status.

God will not abandon you (see Josh. 1:5); He will

always be with you, in all kinds of adversity (see Ps. 46:1). And this relationship is meant to last.

In your marriage it is not enough to simply make room for God; without Him as central to your marriage, the relationship is *incomplete*.

Christian marriage is often pictured as a triangle: man and woman at the base, with God at the apex. As the couple moves closer to God, they move closer to each other. God created the concept of marriage and He helps to make it work.

God planned it so He could be an integral part of the marriage process of growing, learning, and loving. Yet, He must be invited to participate.

Couples need interaction, not just with each other but also with God. The couple already knows that if they are in agreement, their oneness helps them. When they ask God to be a part of their union, the marriage relationship is *fully complete* and can withstand the stresses and adversity that pull at their marriage.

"A cord of three strands is not quickly broken," wrote Solomon in Ecclesiastes 4:12. If you invite the Lord to join your marriage, it will endure.

THE LORD CAN BECOME YOUR PARTNER

Each morning Harriet and I have a quiet time together before starting our day. We enjoy coffee as we chat. I may read a chapter of Scripture or a devotional page. We pray for each other, our children, and our day ahead.

Proverbs is my favorite book of the Bible. It's packed with wisdom, giving us the mind of God on how to live. There are 31 chapters of Proverbs, exactly enough for a month. Each chapter is full of insight, and since there's no plot line, if I skip a day, it doesn't matter.

There are countless devotional books and tapes to help you focus daily upon God. *Heirs Together of Life* is one such book. Charles and Norma Ellis suggest the man do the devotional reading, followed by a sharing of mutual thoughts and reactions, closing with each person praying.

Quiet Times for Couples is another popular daily devotional. H. Norman Wright combines his experience as a psychologist and counselor with the spiritual insights of a biblical scholar, and the authoritative writing of a journalist.

Wright notes that we live in a "hurry up and get there" society which does not welcome waiting upon the Lord (Isa. 40:31). He says there are times when it is best to say to one another, "Let's pray about this and wait upon God for an answer." Have you tried that recently?

That's exactly how Harriet and I treat our toughest decisions. And that's the process which makes the Lord a third partner of our marriage. We once had a difficult choice to make about whether to move from Connecticut to Maryland. So we took the matter to the Lord in prayer and daily discussion. We left the results to Him. We decided to move, and everything worked out just as He promised it would (see Rom. 8:28).

There is no end to the satisfaction, joy, and sense of completeness a couple can have when they **make God a partner** in their marriage.

Biblical References
Job 11:18-19; Proverbs 1:33; 3:24; Isaiah 40:31; Jeremiah 29:12; John 15:5, 7; James 5:16

Other Resources
1. An abundance of devotional materials for couples can be found at your Christian bookstore.

2. *Restoring a Loving Marriage* (David C. Cook, 1989), chapters 9 and 10.

---

[1]Dobson, *Love for a Lifetime*, 53-54.

A N S W E R   17

Insuring Marriage

Experience an Enrichment Weekend to Revive and Strengthen Your Marriage

Virtually every marriage can be made better by attending a structured marriage enrichment retreat. Good marriages can become great ones!

Harriet and I had a good marriage, but in 1976 it was once under great stress. My work in Connecticut was over and I'd gotten a job in Washington. I'd board a train in Stamford at 2 a.m. Mondays, roll into Washington, work all week, and come home exhausted Friday night, arriving at 11 p.m.

Harriet tolerated this schedule graciously for months, even preparing a lovely late dinner Fridays. On Saturdays and Sundays I was buried in writing. I was *not* a good father or husband. During those months, friends at church began suggesting, "Why don't you and Harriet go on a Marriage Encounter weekend?"

I asked, "What is it?" They were mysterious. "It's a way to strengthen your marriage."

Miffed, I retorted, "I *have* a good marriage."

"But Marriage Encounter is designed to make a good marriage better!" As I thought about it, it seemed like a good idea, but when I mentioned it to Harriet, she said, "No!" rather sharply. "Besides, we can't afford it," Harriet added. So I repeated that excuse the next time someone suggested our going. "But your way is already paid for. Go, and we'll even baby-sit your kids."

Harriet was now out of excuses, so we drove 80 miles to a motel, arriving for dinner on Friday. Our first surprise was that every couple who had urged us to go was already there! They had decorated the place with balloons and presented us a basket of fruit.

After dinner, three couples made the first of many intimate presentations, drawing from the experience of their own marriages.

We then returned to our motel room assigned to write the first of many "love letters"—describing what we liked about our spouse and our marriage. Then we exchanged the letters and discussed them privately.

TV sets were unplugged, and we put away all watches to totally focus on each other. Suddenly I was glad I was there spending time alone with Harriet.

The talks from the leader couples were often deeply moving. Father Bob, an Episcopal priest, confessed, "I was married to my job." (I winced, for that sounded exactly like me!) He continued, "I gave little time to Susan. The parish was my world."

When Susan spoke, she was weeping, "A conspiracy kept me from my husband. It is as if he were born with a two-way radio, responding to everyone but his wife. I was ignored."

Later, we were asked to write a "love letter" to our spouse concerning something "that I couldn't or didn't share." I was shocked by Harriet's letter. She wrote that she felt bruised by my work in Washington. "You left me for a year and a half quite voluntarily. I felt deserted." Then, when we discussed the letters, she added, "This is NO marriage.

I never see you during the week—you work all the time and don't even spend time with the boys. This isn't why I married you. You're a workaholic. You love your work, not me."

I broke down and cried. I was so absorbed in the difficulties of my life and work that I hadn't realized its impact on Harriet. I asked her for forgiveness. I didn't know she'd held such deep, burning anger within her all those months.

That experience taught me that our Marriage Encounter leaders were right, **it's essential to take time out with your spouse every day**.

Harriet and I fell back in love that weekend. Our experience is not rare. Some 30 studies report that 80 to 90 percent of the 1.5 million Marriage Encounter attendees found a new joy in their marriage.

There are other effective weekend retreats also designed to refresh a marriage. Some 16,000 attend Festivals of Marriage each year. The theme changes each year, always focusing on a specific issue. Sixty percent of attendees return each year.

Marriage Enrichment is a weekend retreat started by David and Vera Mace. These events are attended by some 18,000 couples each year.

A Weekend to Remember is another such event, attended by over 22,000 couples each year. It is part of the Family Life Ministries of Campus Crusade For Christ.

These marriage renewal and retreat weekends are so intense and meaningful that they are often life-changing.

Larry Lewis, President of the Home Mission Board of the Southern Baptist Convention, attended a Protestant version of Marriage Encounter and said "We naively believed we had no need for any such experience since our marriage was so happy. However, very few, if any, weekends before or since, have been more blessed and meaningful."

Dr. James Dobson confesses that he attended "for professional reasons, not expecting to get anything relevant to my wife and me. If there is anything I felt that Shirley and I didn't need, it was help in communicating. I have rarely been more wrong. Marriage Encounter gave Shirley and me the deepest, most intimate exchange of feelings we had known in 20 years. . . . It proved to be one of the highlights of my life."

Talk to anyone who has attended a weekend marriage retreat, and you will be given a similar response. You owe it to your own marriage to schedule such an event. You might consider paying another couple's way as a gift to their marriage. Either way, it's an investment that will pay on-going dividends.

Biblical References
Psalm 32:8; Isaiah 46:11; Acts 20:35; 1 Timothy 6:6; Hebrews 12:1-2

Other Resources
1. **Marriage Encounter**, call 1-800-795-LOVE or write: Worldwide Marriage Encounter, 1908 E. Highland, #A, San Bernardino, CA 92404.

2. **Marriage Enrichment**, call 1-800-634-8325 or write P.O. Box 10596, Winston-Salem, NC 27108.

3. **A Weekend to Remember**, call 1-501-223-8663 or write: Family Life Ministries, P.O. Box 23840, Little Rock, AR 72221.

4. **Festival of Marriage**, call 1-615-251-2277 or write: Festival of Marriage, 127 Ninth Ave. North, Nashville, TN 37234.

5. *Marriage Savers* by Michael McManus (Zondervan, 1993), chapter 9.

6. *Marriage Savers Resource Collection*, video program 4.

A N S W E R   1 8

Insuring Marriage

Try These 17 Steps for Deeply Troubled Marriages

Couples whose own marriages once nearly failed are uniquely qualified to help marriages in trouble. In 1987 Father Dick McGinnis of St. David's Episcopal Church in Jacksonville, Florida, made an announcement to his congregation, "I want to meet after the service with people whose marriages have been on the rocks, but who have successfully come off of them—people who have been in extreme difficulty and have threatened divorce, but who are in recovery."

To his surprise ten couples showed up. He confessed to them, "I have more marriage counseling than I can handle. There is no way to keep up with it. I prayed about it. What came to me was I was not to look at the problem, but at the solution."

He recalled how Alcoholics Anonymous got started, with "Bill" and "Dr. Bob" helping each other stay sober. So they began helping other alcoholics. AA then developed the "12 Steps" that have helped millions stay sober.

Father McGinnis met with seven of those ten couples over time to see if there was a common thread for marriages to be restored. The couples shared openly and deeply. Father McGinnis asked each, "What did you do to restore your marriage?"

At first their stories seemed radically different. However, there was much in common. Six of the seven had been to Marriage Encounter. More important, each went through certain similar spiritual steps that enabled them to rebuild their marriages.

MARRIAGE MINISTRY

After months of review, the couples worked out what ultimately became *17 Marriage Ministry Action Statements*.

For example, each made a "commitment to follow Jesus as my Savior and Lord," as one story illustrates. Lowell said, "We had tried humanistic books like *I'm OK. You're OK.* None of it was working. So we said, 'Why not try God? What else have we got to lose?' We went to St. David's. We became 'born again' We realized the Lord really loved us and we began to love ourselves." Accepting Christ was the starting point to their restored marriage.

Franki, Lowell's wife, added, "I realized that the problem was with *myself.* I needed to change." She explained, "I was head of the house in everything and he just followed. He did football and the garbage. He left his laundry on the floor. He did not help discipline the kids." Then she saw part of the problem was her sharp tongue. She'd been nagging constantly before she made a commitment to Christ. When she changed, Lowell noticed immediately. "She stopped complaining!" So he was motivated to pick up his clothes—which was a kind act that she noticed and caused her to be more affectionate that night. He even decided to assume the responsibility to discipline the kids.

Franki learned *she could not change her mate. But with God's help she could change.* And remarkably, *her change prompted him to change.* What was before a downward spiral reversed itself.

As the seven couples shared their stories, their own marriages improved. Those seven couples have now worked with 40 other couples whose marriages were deeply troubled, and there's been only one separation! That's a 98 percent success rate!

In Ephesians 4:12, the Apostle Paul says the job of a pastor is "to prepare God's people for works of service." What greater need is there in every church than saving marriages?

Over half of America's marriages fail. Father McGinnis reflects, "I started this looking to see if God had a way for marriages to be restored. He does. It's summed up in the 17 Marriage Ministry Steps. Any pastor could use them to equip recovering couples to help others. The couples' personal experience breathes life into the steps."

Marriage Ministry 17 Steps

1. Through other Christians, find hope for our marriage.

2. Personally experience God's love and forgiveness.

3. Make a personal decision/commitment to love: Christ, mate, self.

4. Make a decision/commitment to follow Christ as Savior and Lord.

5. Once obedient to God, begin to love by His standards, not ours.

6. Become accountable to God for my behavior, thoughts, and actions, and become aware of accountability to others.

7. Make a decision to stay together.

8. Make a decision to forgive my mate and myself.

9. Accept my mate as he/she is.

10. Realize that the problem was with myself.

11. Begin to look at myself as needing to change to be able to love, no matter what. Become aware that I need to change, become willing to change, learn

what and how to change; begin change with God's help.

12. Make an examination of my role in marriage according to God's Word and change accordingly with God's help.

13. Accept change in my mate.

14. Through Christ, begin trusting enough to increasingly put whole self in the care of my mate.

15. Learn to communicate honestly and openly in love.

16. Learn to put God and mate ahead of self (humble before the Lord).

17. Realize we are still in process, that we must share what we have found with others.

Biblical References

Ephesians 4:12; 5:21-33; Philippians 2:1-4; 1 Corinthians 13:4-6

Other Resources

1. *Marriage Savers* by Michael McManus (Zondervan, 1993), chapter 10.

2. *Marriage Savers Resource Collection,* video program 5.

3. See the *Marriage Savers Leader's Study Guide* for help on how to start such a ministry in your church.

A N S W E R   1 9

Consider Retrouvaille for Deeply Troubled Marriages

Divorce is devastating. Divorce affects the couple involved, their extended families, and children they may have. Divorce creates a series of events that brings chaos into many lives. Divorce can be avoided. *Even deeply troubled marriages can be restored to health*. The most dramatic and successful initiative to pull marriages from divorce courts was created in Quebec by Catholic lay leaders of Marriage Encounter who observed that the weekend retreat was not reaching many of those couples already headed toward divorce.

They designed a new weekend, followed by six additional sessions, led by mentor couples whose *own* marriages had once nearly dissolved. Called "Retrouvaille" (French for "Rediscovery", pronounced ret-roo-vie), the movement is now in 100 metropolitan areas of the United States.

Its results are spectacular. In Fort Worth, Texas, 40 percent of 817 couples attending *were already separated*. Yet, *70 percent have rebuilt their marriages!* In Buffalo, New York, the success rate was 93 percent.

Retrouvaille attendees must agree in advance that they want to make their marriage work. And, if a third party is involved, that outside affair or relationship must end.

Leader couples share with attendees how they nearly destroyed their own marriages. One man, Bob Pate, confessed his affairs. But Marie, his wife, admitted "I never faced *my responsibility* for his unfaithfulness."

Leaders explain, "Love is a decision, not a feeling. Feelings come and go. Love as a decision gives us control over ourselves."

After each lecture, attendees return to their rooms with an assignment to write out their feelings. Afterwards, they exchange notebooks, read, and talk privately.

They repeat this intensive process over a weekend, and lay a foundation for healing. Then they meet at least six more times with other "graduates."

Two of those who heard Bob and Marie share their story were Mike and Brenda. A traveling computer expert, Mike had frequented bars and picked up women for brief affairs.

He got away with it for years until he had a fling with a woman whose husband found out and confronted him as did Mike's wife, Brenda. Shocked and angry, she said, "I wanted to kill. If I would have had a gun in my hand, he would not be alive. It was horrible." Their screaming confrontation took place in front of their boys, ages nine and six. The frightened, tearful children had never even seen them argue before!

How did Retrouvaille help? Brenda and Mike saw other couples who—like them—had been through much misery in their lives. They heard firsthand how they'd come through it. Hearing such success stories is *genuinely motivating.* It makes couples want the same happiness in their marriage.

Retrouvaille leads to healed marriages by using other couples who have overcome troubled marriages. This effective process equips these couples with communication tools and the loving heart to continue to work on their marriages. And the process cycle begins again with other couples.

Four years after Brenda and Mike's experience with Retrouvaille, their teenage son, Jason, wrote them an anniversary letter: "Thank you for being mine and Jacob's parents, and all you do for me. You stayed together mostly because you did not want to lose us or hurt us, and we respect you for making that decision."

Biblical References

Psalm 42:11; 71:20; Isaiah 55:7; Ephesians 5:21-33; 1 John 1:7-9; 3:20

Other Resources

1. For information about **Retrouvaille,** call Roger and Pat Bate (713) 455-1656.

2. *Marriage Savers* by Michael McManus (Zondervan, 1993), chapter 10.

3. *Marriage Savers Resource Collection,* video program 5.

Consider Reconciliation If You Are Separated or Divorced

Even when a marriage is torn asunder, it is possible—and important—to achieve a level of reconciliation. Are you divorced, separated, or likely to be one of 1.2 million couples who split apart this year? If you are not, no doubt you know a couple that will join those ranks. There is hope. One answer is reconciliation.

Mention the word **"reconciliation"** to an angry, separated spouse, and the likely response is "No way! I don't want to have anything to do with him/her." Even so, Dr. Jim Talley suggests, "It's *never* too late!" He should know. He's worked with 13,000 "singles" over the past 25 years, many of whom were once married.

The normal assumption is that it is unlikely or impossible to achieve reconciliation. Talley observes that, "The model American marital advice of pastors and friends comes in five words: 'Get on with your life.' In other words, forget your spouse. Find someone else."

Problems aren't solved by divorcing and remarrying. Second marriages have a 60 percent divorce rate. Why? "You tend to drag all the diffi-culties of the first marriage into the second," ob-serves Talley. "The tendency is to choose the same character deficiencies in the second partner as the first. I have seen people marry three alcoholics in a row."

Fortunately, "Reconciliation Instruction" has helped hundreds of couples restore harmony, love, and marriage to once hopeless relationships.

More than half of those who are separated and take the course are able to save their marriages. And even most others who do divorce are able to re-store a sense of civility to their relationships.

The prime time to offer Reconciliation Instruction is immediately after the separation, and before ei-ther person has begun dating again. In fact, a pre-requisite to taking the four-month reconciliation course is an agreement by both people not to date anyone else.

There are other prerequisites:

1. No changes are to be made in the legal status of the relationship. If you are living separately, con-tinue to do so.

2. Do not talk or even think about remarriage during the four months, to protect the relationship from unrealistic expectations.

3. Limit the physical relationship to the lowest level desired by either partner.

The course also can be taken by divorced cou-ples. However, Talley warns, "Reconciliation does not necessarily mean remarriage. At first it may only mean reducing the danger level when children are exchanged for visits," (when some couples have their most violent arguments).

The primary goal is to enable those who are angry, bitter, and hostile to be friendly again. It's possible to bring back harmony, whether separated, divorced, or remarried.

The course requires reading *Reconcilable Differences,* writing in a workbook, and meeting with your partner eight times to read and discuss what each has written. Finally, they must attend eight sessions with an instructor or mentor couple.

Mary heard about the course in church. Immature and only 19 when she married Bob, she was very submissive, which he, a corporate climber, enjoyed. But as three children came along, she changed. Mary became assertive, which Bob didn't like, so he buried himself in a 12 to 15 hour work day. "I felt completely out of his life, and perceived there must be another woman," Mary says.

Bob recalls, "I was a workaholic, no husband at all, a money-maker. Communication stopped. What caused separation was my temper got out of hand. There was no physical abuse, but only because I restrained myself."

Mary told him to leave and he did, but continued paying the bills.

She was bitter, depressed, and felt utterly hopeless when she began Reconciliation Instruction. Her feelings were natural. Mary invited Bob to the course. At first, he declined, but later said, "What hit home with me was she found a peace in what we were going through, and I was on a roller coaster."

Mary's one-sided change made her very attractive to Bob. So he attended and asked to move back in. Mary and her counselor said no, that Bob had to take four months of Reconciliation Instruction first.

Bob was furious. "I want to move in with my wife, and then take the course."

The counselor explained, "The success rate is dramatically improved if you remain apart."

Bob reluctantly agreed. Then "lights turned on" for him; he got his spiritual life together. The most important lesson from the course was learning the skills of how to resolve conflict. Bob and Mary are now back together in a growing marriage.

What should you do when your spouse won't take the course? "First," says Talley, "Stabilize your life spiritually, emotionally, lovingly, and financially. Second, sit still and wait. Do not date, so that when the other person cycles back (and most do) you are a more mature, stable person and available to respond." Talley says that the other person is enticed to come back by the fragrance of your changed life.

Changed people are able to change people.

Biblical References
James 1:19-20; Psalm 37:8; Ephesians 4:31-32; Colossians 3:8; Proverbs 16:7; Hebrews 13:6

Other Resources
1. *Reconcilable Differences* by Jim Talley, (Thomas Nelson Publishers, 1991)

2. *Reconciliation Instruction Workbooks,* published by Jim Talley, available by calling (405) 789-2900.

3. *How to Reconcile a Marriage,* one-hour audio tape from Focus on the Family, with Dr. James Dobson, Jim Talley and two couples whose marriages he helped restore. Write Focus on the Family, Colorado Springs, CO 80995.

4. *Marriage Savers Resource Collection,* video program 6.

5. *Divorce Recovery* by Harold Ivan Smith (Broadman & Holman, 1994).

Insuring
Marriage

*Stepfamily Support Groups
Provide Mutual Help
and Encouragement*

United Methodist Singles Pastor Dick Dunn of the
Atlanta area didn't pay much attention to Joe and
Carla Martin when they asked him for help with
their tumultuous stepparent family. After all, the
couple was from the church—surely there would
be no real problems in their second marriage. Or so
he thought.

However, Dick recalled the explosion that occurred after his own divorce when his daughter,
Kim, came home from college one Christmas. Dick
and his second wife Betty, had just moved to the
Atlanta area. When his daughter arrived for the hol-
idays, Dick took several days showing Kim all the
sights. But Betty felt like a fifth wheel.

Betty labored over the Christmas turkey, but
when she was ready to serve it, Kim was listening
to rock music. "Would you please put on Christmas
carols?" Betty asked.

Not only was Kim's answer "No," but Dick sided
with her. "Why not let her play her music?"

The next day, Dick said to Betty, "Kim and I want
to eat Chinese. Do you want to go with us?"

Betty retorted, "No. And I won't be here when you get back. I'm going back home to Ohio."

That got Dick's attention. Like many divorced fathers who see their kids occasionally, Dick didn't see the problem with his daughter's behavior and didn't realize he was neglecting his wife whenever Kim was around.

Dick resolved his immediate crisis, then remembered the Martin's plea for help. He created a "Stepfamily Support Group." The group has helped more than 200 couples discover that they aren't alone in facing severe conflict.

Joe and Carla shared their story at the group's first meeting—how they'd expected "bliss and a new family" not "constant fighting and bickering." "It was the most painful experience I have ever been through. I set deadlines. If it's not better in six months, I'll not put up with it any longer," Carla said. "When his kids visited on weekends, Joe didn't discipline them since he only saw them a few days a week." His son Brian now admits that he did things "to purposely drive Carla crazy." Joe recalls, "I never wanted to believe anything bad about my kids."

Sally and Van Malone remember the shock of their first Christmas. Each had both a boy and girl from a previous marriage, and the four kids seemed to get along well before the wedding. Their vision was a "Brady Bunch" family.

But that first Christmas was a horror. They discovered that three different mini-family traditions and three separate timetables had to be negotiated: Van and his kids; Sally and hers; Sally's ex-husband and his new wife who lived nearby. Conflicts between the three families were fierce.

Van was a widower whose first wife died of cancer. His daughter Rachel assumed the leadership role of her mother and ran their household for five years—during the two years her mother was sick and died, and afterward, when her father was a single parent.

Rachel was unwilling to give her father up to this new woman. Right after the honeymoon, she announced, "I don't want another mother." When Sally went to take a shower, Rachel would take *her* shower, draining the hot water. "She treated me like a piece of furniture, talking only to Van, never to me," said Sally.

Rachel accused her dad, "You never really loved my mother." She reasoned, "If Dad loves Sally, he never loved Mom."

Fortunately, Roswell's Stepfamily Support Group had already been organized when Sally and Van married. After a few months of marriage they shared with the support group their experience of conflict with Rachel and the other kids and Sally's ex-husband.

"It sounds *normal* to us," a chorus replied.

That was a great relief to hear," Sally recalls. People think what they are experiencing is unique to them. In stepfamilies the finger of blame gets pointed at everyone—with no one realizing that stepparent-stepchild-biological parent conflict is normal.

Roswell's stepfamily group has now worked with 200 couples in turmoil, only 10 of whom got divorced. That's only a *5 percent divorce* rate for those in second marriages compared to a normal 60 percent!

"It saved our marriage," many say. How? Dick Dunn outlines lessons in *Willing To Try Again: Steps Toward Blending a Family.*

1. Changing rules: Single parent households tend to be lax on rules and kids help shape them. Blended families return to rules imposed by parents, sparking explosions. Go slowly in changing rules.

2. Time with parent: Single parents who once

spent hours with children tend to spend no time with them after the marriage. That is unwise.

3. The "wicked" stepparent: The biological parent must elevate the importance of the stepparent. If kids ask a father permission to do something, he can say, "Let me check with Sue." That involves his partner. Later he can say, "Sue thinks it makes sense," creating goodwill in the mind of the child because of the stepparent's approval.

4. Family conferences: Stepfamilies often meet weekly, giving each person a chance to say anything, respectful or not. "I don't like you," a stepson might say.

Sue might respond, "But we live together. Let's work things out in a way we can both accept."

5. Couple time alone: Couples must continue to have "dates" and weekend getaways without kids, to nurture their own relationship.

6. Create stepfamily groups: Every church should form a stepfamily support group.

Couples who have remarried and who have the problems of stepchildren, ex-spouses, and the clashes of stepfamilies need to take steps to deal with these problem areas. *Nothing could do more to save second marriages from second divorces.*

Biblical References
Psalm 121:7-8; 1 Corinthians 10:13; Hebrews 10:35-36; 12:14; James 1:3-6; 1 Peter 3:13; 1 John 4:11

Other Resources
1. Contact the Stepfamily Association of America for help organizing a support group (402) 477-STEP.

2. *Marriage Savers Resource Collection,* video program 6, features Rev. Dick Dunn's Stepfamily Support Group.

3. *Willing To Try Again: Steps Toward Blending a Family* by Dick Dunn (Judson Press, 1993).

Insuring Marriage

Single Adults — Insuring Their Future Marriages and Being Marriage Savers

Single adult Christians should help transform their church into a place that helps them develop and provide programs and activities for building up other single adults and couples while helping to create lifelong marriages.

Many adults in most churches are single, but few are in church leadership, maybe because their priority is in finding a lifelong mate. But those singles fail to realize that *the church could be their best ally* in that task, especially when their leadership service consists of helping other single adults (never marrieds and formerly marrieds) find answers to their questions about marriage.

Being single is as valid a biblical model for Christian service as being married. Jesus, Paul, and Martha were unmarried. But since many church single adults want to marry, they need to be involved in understanding the marriage relationship.

QUESTIONS FOR A SINGLE ADULT GATHERING

Why not have your next single adult retreat or seminar focus on tough marital questions? Some could be based on the Answers reported in this book.

1. What can help single adults avoid a bad marriage?

Chastity increases the odds of a lifelong marriage by two-thirds. Are you committed to not "live together"? How can you build a good marriage, or understand what's wrong with divorce?

Help your church promote an abstinence campaign in which teenagers and single adults promise God that they will be sexually pure. How can your church also offer help to seriously dating couples? Ask for a similar pledge of chastity so they can build a relationship on God. Relationship Instruction includes such a pledge.

Does your church offer PREPARE, the premarital inventory that can predict whether a marriage will end in divorce? The best time to take it is when a seriously dating couple is trying to decide whether to marry.

Single adults can provide real leadership in this area, but may even benefit from it as well, since PREPARE's creators say the best time to take this inventory is when the singles who make up the couple have not yet decided to marry.

2. How can our church insure future marriages?

See to it that your church offers its seriously dating singles some kind of Relationship Instruction. While half who take it do not marry, of those who do, more than 90 percent have a lasting marriage. *That's real "Marriage Insurance!"*

Is your church's premarital program rigorous? Is it mandatory? Are mature married mentor couples involved? Are there lectures and classes for dating singles on tough marital issues: managing money, sex in marriage, conflict resolution, communication? Are engaged couples taught biblical principles?

Is there a minimum time for marriage preparation? Does your church encourage engaged couples to attend a retreat? If your church offers these proven steps to single adults who become engaged, their odds of a lifelong marriage increase dramatically.

Of course, none of these steps will help you, as a single adult, to find the right person! At least not directly. But if your church is known as a place that cherishes single adults so much that it takes serious steps to help unmarried people build a lifelong marriage, your congregation will attract a larger number of single adults and people who are, like you, deeply committed to spiritual values. And from this company of singles, many may meet a life partner.

3. Does our church have a special focus on those who are "single again"—separated or divorced?

Those who are "single again" after a separation or divorce have special needs that are different from single adults who have never been married. For example, a recently separated person should not be encouraged to date. Retrouvaille and Reconciliation Instruction are programs that can save more than half of separated marriages, and even reunite some of the already divorced couples. Separated persons are still married and churches should use these programs to provide possible rebonding by separated husbands and wives.

Finally, you can offer divorced single adults "divorce recovery" classes that can help a new single-again person rebuild the self-esteem that's inevitably shattered by separation and divorce.

Biblical References
Proverbs 2:5-7; Ecclesiastes 2:26; Matthew 16:24; Hebrews 11:6; James 1:12

Other Resources

1. *Christian Single* magazine (product # 1806). Order by calling 1-800-458-2772 or write Customer Service Center; 127 Ninth Avenue, North; Nashville, TN 37234.

2. *A Time for Healing: Coming to Terms with Your Divorce* by Harold Ivan Smith (LifeWay Press, 1994).

3. *Willing To Try Again* by Dick Dunn (Judson Press, 1993).

4. *Marriage Savers Resource Collection,* video program 6.

5. Focus on the Family single parents' magazine. Call (719) 531-5181.

6. To receive a packet on organizing a single adult ministry, contact: Single Adult Ministry; (MSN 151); 127 Ninth Avenue, North; Nashville, TN 37234.

7. *Singles Adult Ministries Journal,* P.O. Box 62056, Colorado Springs, CO 80962-2056.

Insuring
Marriage

Participating in Church Can Help Save a Marriage

Pollsters have said that people who participate in church on a regular basis have better results in social and personal relationships. The strength that comes from being actively involved in a church family has been well documented.

People who attend church tend to live longer, happier, and more productive lives. They have inner strength that helps them cope with life's stresses. There is a common unity and single focus of faith that brings men and women together. For thousands of years, churches have provided purpose and common values.

Because of strong moral and ethical values among those who are church members, single adults who are seeking a mate are more likely to be satisfied with the choices they find at church.

Church has become a place of refuge, a home for us to commune with "brothers and sisters" who are like-minded.

While not perfect, our churches still offer more hope than any other institution to those who face unusual problems and difficulties in life or society. That's why those who are looking for a marriage partner or facing marital difficulties should be attending church.

The spiritual strength that is obtained from an attachment to a church can make a difference in how well a person does in selecting a mate or how well marriage difficulties can be resolved. Church fellowship, prayer, and pastoral counsel are not usually available outside the church. The vital sources of emotional and spiritual strength found in a church can make a significant difference for those who are in the throes of divorce.

Yet, we know that the divorce rate among church members is nearly the same as society in general. And not all pastors and their congregations are well equipped to help their members deal with divorce.

Even strong churches with a myriad of ministries often do nothing to strengthen existing marriages or save troubled ones. Indeed, some even separate married couples. My church has a men's retreat and a women's retreat, but only newlyweds have couples' retreats. Harriet and I are working to organize a Marriage Encounter weekend for all interested married couples.

The initiative has to come from couples like you and Harriet and me, with a heart for strengthening marriage. What does your church do to help newlyweds succeed? Half of the newly wed are horrified by the conflicts they are experiencing. Is there a **mentoring program** available for them?

Are **marriage classes** offered to small groups— even three or four couples—for an objective view of their strengths and areas for needed growth. Is there a **Bible Study** for newlyweds?

Has every married couple been urged to attend Marriage Encounter, Marriage Enrichment, or a Festival of Marriage **weekend retreat** to make their marriage better? If not, why not? Why don't you go?

If your experience is powerful, you'll be an effective advocate for church-wide change.

Many churches are helping singles and couples get help for **marriage preparation** or **counseling**. An Assembly of God church in Illinois puts $5,000 into its budget to pay for a Valentine's weekend for every couple. Should this be a part of your church's budget? If marriage is the bedrock institution of our society, it deserves support in both money and time.

Our church recruits couples with 20-50 years of successful marital experience to **mentor younger couples**. Harriet and I have trained 22 other couples who are investing themselves in the lives of seriously dating couples, engaged, and newlyweds. It is a joyous ministry, and one that deepens the marriages of those of us who are mentors as much as those we mentor.

Many churches offer **courses to strengthen marriage**, such as the *Covenant Marriage* courses of the Sunday School Board. Those also provide great training for mentors.

Other churches have developed **plans to intervene** with couples on the verge of divorce and save some of the most deeply troubled marriages. Father Dick McGinnis, an Episcopal minister in Florida, created a support group similar to Alcoholics Anonymous that is designed to rescue and heal marriages. His story was told in Answer 18.

Other church leaders can offer this ministry for an effective reduction in the divorce rate in their churches. Or they can develop their own principles. Ask couples who have survived bad marriages if they would help couples currently in trouble.

Father McGinnis' 7 couples have worked with 40 troubled marriages in Jacksonville since 1987 and none have divorced, though one did separate. Your church can have such a healing ministry that can save seemingly hopeless marriages.

Retrouvaille is a **weekend retreat for couples with marital problems** that brings hope and healing to still other couples (see Answer 19).

Even if divorce has already occurred, your church can minister to you. Many churches have established **divorce recovery workshops** and **support groups**, providing a loving, Christian community for healing.

There are **support groups for helping second marriages**, such as the Stepfamily Support Group established by Roswell United Methodist Church in Georgia.

For a long time, churches ignored the need to help young people choose the right marriage partner, prepare them with instruction, and address the problems of troubled marriages. These churches simply refused to acknowledge that Christians were divorcing in about the same numbers as the rest of society. But now, more than ever, **the church is the place to go for encouragement, support, and spiritual reinforcement.** Churches can and should be marriage savers.

Biblical References

2 Chronicles 15:2; Isaiah 58:9; Acts 17:27; Colossians 3:12-13; Titus 2:1-5; Hebrews 11:6

Other Resources

1. *Finding A Church You Can Call Home: a Complete Guide to Making One of the Most Important Decisions of Your Life* by George Barna, (Regal Books, 1992).

2. *Marriage Savers Resource Collection,* video program 1.

3. *Marriage Savers* by Michael McManus (Zondervan, 1993), chapters 7 and 10.

4. *Covenant Marriage: Partnership and Commitment* by Diana Garland and Betty Hassler (LifeWay Press, 1989).

5. *Communication and Intimacy: Covenant Marriage* by Gary Chapman and Betty Hassler (LifeWay Press, 1992).

6. *I Take Thee to Be My Spouse,* compiled by David Apple (Convention Press, 1992).

7. *A Time for Healing: Coming to Terms with Your Divorce* by Harold Ivan Smith (LifeWay Press, 1994).

A N S W E R 2 4

Insuring Marriage

Work Toward Revising State Laws to Insure Marriages

State government should not grant marriage licenses without evidence that a couple has had premarital counseling and testing to increase the odds their marriage will last.

State marital law in every state works against efforts to provide effective marriage preparation. State laws send the opposite and wrong messages to people:

• Teen marriages are encouraged.

Every state allows those 18 years of age and older to marry without parental consent. But many age restrictions fall well below that. With parental permission, a *girl of 12* or a *boy of 14* can marry in Massachusetts. In New Hampshire, it is 13 and 14, respectively. Most other states allow marriages at 16. Think of the strikes against the marriage when children are allowed to marry.

• Marriages of impulse are encouraged.

A couple that applies for a marriage license has *no waiting period* in half of the 50 United States! Most other states require only a three-day delay. The longest wait is just five days.

• Testing is not required.

Although most states require blood tests for

venereal disease (but not AIDS) they do not test the couple's readiness to marry and start a family.

• No premarital counseling is required by any state.

What sense does this make? Every state in America asks a person who wants a driver's license to pass three tests: a written test on the law; a practical, hands-on driving test; and an eye test. But no counseling or test is required to marry.

Present state law encourages quick weddings, as if deliberation in the choice of a lifelong mate were unimportant. Yet the cost of divorce to the state is immense.

Most state marriage laws remain unchanged after more than a century. In fact, *the only change has been for the worse.* Before the 1970s, a male under age 21 who wanted to marry had to have the permission of his parents. Now he can marry at 18 *without permission,* or 14 to 16 with it. How many 17-year-olds today are mature enough to choose a partner for life?

SEEK MINIMUM STATE REQUIREMENTS

Marriage should not be a light decision, made when young hormones are speaking louder than cool judgment. Rather, it should be a mature decision— agreed on by both parties and deliberated over time.

We are not realistic if we expect a state government to be as demanding as a church. However, states can require a two-month waiting period to obtain a marriage license in order to allow time for marriage preparation.

Why shouldn't states *require* a couple to present some *kind of certification* indicating they've had premarital testing, counseling, and training? The certificate could be signed by a secular counselor or by the pastor of a church.

If the state had a minimum two-month requirement for a marriage license, churches and synagogues could easily require and expect four months of marriage preparation.

State divorce laws also need to be changed. In 47 states, one person can unilaterally dissolve a marriage, even if the other person wants to reconcile. What is worse the "innocent" party often ends up subsidizing the person "guilty" of marital misconduct.

Consider taking on an advocacy role in seeking some basic marriage law reforms for your state. A call to your state representative with these concerns might open the door to effective reform in your state.

In addition to saving marriages, states will realize untold millions of dollars in not having to subsidize the social ills resulting from divorce.

State governments should not grant marriages without evidence that a couple is ready for it.

Biblical References
Psalm 106:3; 2 Corinthians 5:20; Philippians 4:8; James 4:17

Other Resources
1. *Marriage Savers* by Michael McManus (Zondervan, 1993), chapters 7 and 11.

Insuring Marriage

Help Create a Community Marriage Policy

Pastors from 20 denominations in 25 cities have started reforms in many churches to radically reduce the divorce rate and been successful in saving thousands of marriages.

Being married by a pastor should have greater meaning than being married by a justice of the peace. But sadly, six in ten new marriages are failing despite the fact that 75 percent of the marriages are blessed by churches.

However, some churches truly are blessings to couples. This book has pointed to pioneering answers from the three great streams of Christianity in America: Catholic, evangelical, and mainline Protestantism.

But the churches are not learning from each other. Catholic churches require engaged couples to take a premarital inventory; meet with older, mentor couples with solid marriages; and have a minimum number of months of marriage preparation. An Episcopal church created a Marriage Ministry that saved 39 of 40 deeply troubled marriages. A United Methodist Church pioneered strategies which preserve 95 percent of stepfamilies—a contrast with the usual 60 percent divorce rate of second marriages. Southern Baptists created True Love Waits that prompted hundreds of thousands of teenagers to pledge to be chaste until they marry. Evangelicals are much more likely to ask couples living together to separate before getting married.

Therefore, when I speak to local clergy, I urge pastors of all denominations to consider creating a Community Marriage Policy that blends the best of all of these innovations. My dream is that you, your church, and your community will consider **a covenant that stretches across denominational lines—a commitment by every church in your area to demand more of engaged couples: more time, more testing, more study, and more training. And every church should offer more help to strengthen existing marriages.**

Hundreds of pastors from many denominations in two dozen diverse cities have agreed to start these reforms in a Community Marriage Policy. The result?—There were 1,210 divorces in Peoria County, IL in 1991 when clergy created the Peoria Community Marriage Policy. One year later, the number plunged to 947 divorces! And in 1993 there were only 997. Peoria has seen a one-fifth drop in the divorce rate!

Creating a Community Marriage Policy is not easy. A new resource to help is *Marriage Savers Resource Collection* which includes six videos that can make these reforms visible. Couples tell how various reforms saved their marriages. The *Collection* also includes a *Leader's Study Guide* that can be used for a 13-week adult study, *Marriage Savers*, and a copy of this book. I believe these resources can reduce the divorce rate of any church.

The *Collection* was also designed to help create a Community Marriage Policy. Here are suggestions on how to begin.

1. Ask your pastor to invite a diverse group of pastors to overview the *Collection*. Include

Catholic, mainline Protestant, evangelical, and minority pastors. Give each a copy of *Marriage Savers* and view Video 1.

2. Enlist a group of the most influential religious leaders in your community to join a Community Marriage Policy committee. If the city is large, include bishops, superintendents, or directors of mission who could prompt other pastors to become involved.

3. Encourage committee members to use *Marriage Savers Resource Collection* in their churches. This motivates them to encourage other clergy to come to a city-wide presentation of the Community Marriage Policy idea.

4. Take the initiative to mediate and negotiate the exact content of a Community Marriage Policy. There is no rigid formula. Some guidelines focus only on premarital couples. The newest policies have added guidelines encouraging chastity of teenagers and single adults. The initial task of a Community Marriage Policy committee is to thrash out their own policy.

5. Challenge the committee to enlist pastors from their denominations to attend a city-wide Community Marriage Policy adoption meeting. Experience indicates the biggest problem is getting them **to attend.** Urge as many clergy as possible to sign the policy **that day.**

6. Invite the press to attend the Community Marriage Policy adoption meeting. This is a major local story and should get good coverage. Give the press a list of all those who sign the policy. That alone will encourage many couples to work harder at their marriages, and it will encourage pastors who do not attend to join.

Sample Community Marriage Policy

Preamble

Our concern as ministers is to foster lasting marital unions under God and establish successful spiritual families. Almost 75 percent of all marriages are performed by pastors, and we are troubled by the more than 60 percent divorce rate. Our concern is to radically reduce the divorce rate among those married in area churches.

Pastors have the responsibility to raise the quality of commitment in those we marry. We believe that couples who seriously participate in premarital testing and counseling will have a better understanding of what the marriage commitment involves. As agents of God, acting on His behalf, we feel it is our responsibility to encourage couples to set aside time for marriage preparation. We acknowledge that a wedding is but a day while a marriage is for a lifetime.

We also believe that the church has an ongoing responsibility to help strengthen existing marriages and to save deeply troubled ones. "For I hate divorce, says the Lord God of Israel" (Mal. 2:16). What God has joined together, let the church help hold together.

Community Marriage Policy

1. We will encourage teenagers to sign a True Love Waits pledge and encourage older single adults to practice sexual abstinence.

2. We will offer Relationship Instruction to seriously dating couples.

3. We will require a minimum of four months marriage preparation.

4. We will require six counseling sessions, with two devoted to the use of a premarital inventory, and others on Scripture, and the substantive problems of finances, sex, communication, and conflict resolution.

5. We will train mature, married couples to serve as mentors to work with seriously dating, engaged couples, and newlyweds on a couple-to-couple basis.

6. We will encourage attendance at an Engaged Encounter weekend to help the engaged improve their communications skills, and establish their marriage with God at the center.

7. We will offer two post-marital counseling sessions with clergy or a mentor couple, six months and a year after the wedding.

8. We will encourage all married couples to attend a couple's retreat such as Marriage Encounter, Festival of Marriage, or Marriage Enrichment.

9. We will develop a Marriage Ministry of mentoring couples whose own marriage once failed to work with currently troubled marriages.

10. Those of us who are married will be the first to attend a couples' retreat.

11. We clergy will participate and cooperate fully to learn and experience more about how to help couples bond for life.

12. As clergy, we will take this policy back to our congregations to be ratified by the appropriate boards and/or congregations.

13. We will ask others to evaluate this policy.

14. We will appoint a committee of attorneys to propose changes in the state's laws of marriage and divorce.

Statement of Support

Signed:_____

Congregation:_____

Address:_____

Phone: _____

Biblical References

Deuteronomy 10:12-13; 11:18-19; Psalm 16:11; 106:35-36; Matthew 5:27-32; 1 Timothy 6:11-12

Marriage Savers Declaration

We, _____ **and** _____,
do hereby recommit our vows of marital faithfulness, in thought and deed, and promise before God that we shall stay together, from this
day forward, for better or for worse; for richer
or for poorer; in sickness and in health; to
love, honor and cherish, until death do us
part.

We also pledge our commitment to
strengthen and save the marriages of others,
since God hates divorce, and to establish
Marriage Saver ministries in our church to
help its members:

- Avoid a bad marriage before it begins;
- Give Marriage Insurance to the engaged;
- Strengthen every existing marriage;
- Save even deeply troubled marriages;
- Foster reconciliation between separated
  and divorced members.

Finally, we pledge to encourage our
church to join with other congregations in a
Community Marriage Policy to radically reduce the divorce rate where we live.

*For what God has joined together,
let the church hold together.*

Agreed to by: _____
                          (husband)

            _____
                          (wife)

Date: _____